The Greatest Risk of All

The Greatest Risk of All

Rebekah R. Nash

Warrior Princess Nation, LLC

Copyright © 2021 by Rebekah R. Nash

All rights reserved. No part of this book may be reproduced in any manner whatsoever without written permission except in the case of brief quotations embodied in critical articles and reviews.

All Scripture used is from the NKJV unless otherwise noted.
Scripture taken from the New King James Version. Copyright © 1982 by Thomas Nelson, Inc. Used by permission.

First Printing, 2021

Cover Image: Simply Lynne Photography

For additional information contact the publisher
Warrior Princess Nation
info@warriorprincessnation.com

But what is life without some sort of risk involved? If you live knowing what each day would bring, is that really living at all?

I dedicate this book to my amazing God, my wonderful husband Patrick who gave me the time and inspiration to write this, to my daughter Lily, and to all of my friends and family who have had an incredible impact on my journey. I love you all

Contents

Dedication v

Prologue 1

1. Risk: What is it Exactly? 2
2. Outcomes: Good or Bad 5
3. Hearing from God: How? 10
4. God's Will: What Direction do I go? 16
5. Purpose: Can God use Me? 21
6. Risk #1: High School 26
7. Risk #2: College 34
8. Risk #3 Lilianna Faith 42
9. Risk #4: I Have Had Enough! 51
10. Risk #5: 365 Letters 61
11. Risk #6: Kidney Donation 70
12. Risk #7: Finding Love 86
13. Surrender: The Greatest Risk of All 96

Contents

About The Author 100

Prologue

What is a risk? Is it really worth it, as some might say it is? Do you really experience risk in every step of life that you take? These are all questions I hope to help guide you through as each of you dive into this biography of my life. Life is a whirlwind, and to me, it really is a life worth living. Others may argue that everything is planned for us by some great being, and we don't really have a choice in what we do. So how is anything risky at all? Others may say that we are all accidents, and we can't ever go wrong in what we decide or which route we take. Since we are in control of our own future. I would personally say there is a happy medium that many of us might be missing. Well, at least I know I was missing for a great part of my life.

I have to say, it is very refreshing to be able to do this, and I am excited to see how far God takes this book. The fact that you're reading this, gives me chills, and I am super excited about it! I thank you for being willing to pick this book up and read my story. My prayer is that you absorb anything that God is possibly wanting to speak to you.

So stick around, and I hope that you find some encouragement by the end of this.

{ 1 }

Risk: What is it Exactly?

To establish the worth of risk-taking, let's first look at what this word "risk" is actually defined as. According to Merriam-Webster dictionary, risk can be a noun - "possibility of loss or injury," or a verb - "to expose to hazard or danger." Now let me stop you there really quick. Both of those definitions mention losing something, being injured, or danger. Why is that? Well, if you look closely at the source that the definitions are coming from, it's a dictionary created by man. It's earthly, worldly, so it's dangerous. As humans, we are manipulated to think so much is in danger. Most will label us as crazy or insane if we desire to pursue risks. They focus on the what-ifs, which mainly revolve around the worst-case scenario. Why? I firmly believe that that is what we are taught from the get-go. But I beg to differ. There is another way and another form of risk. The good kind that actually leads to life!

Throughout the Bible, there are examples of risks mentioned, even in the times of Jesus. But there is one particular example found in the Old Testament.

"He who observes the wind will not sow, and he who regards the clouds will not reap. As you do not know the way the spirit comes to the bones in the womb of a woman with child, so you do not know the work of God who makes everything. In the morning sow

The Greatest Risk of All

your seed, and at evening withhold not your hand, for you do not know which will prosper, this or that, or whether both alike will be good." Ecclesiastes 11:4-6

Reading the Bible can be quite difficult for me sometimes, but the beauty of God's word is that it speaks to all of us differently because we are all created with different gifts and thought processes. God can take the same words and use them to speak to us in a way we each understand and interpret them the way we need at that time. Years ago, I don't believe I would have interpreted these verses the way I do today. I would honestly have been confused, but now I read it whenever I am faced with a decision, whether to go out and tend to my garden, put in the work to conceive another child, or whatever it may be. I don't know what the work I put in will bring. Only God knows. I am not the creator of the universe; God is. So who am I to look at a situation through human eyes and determine what I am going to do based on what I think will happen? I could go outside and plant a garden, and nothing come of it—no rain for days, a complete failure. Or I could go outside, and that same garden could produce the fruits and veggies I need for my family for the week. Or even for the month. To me, that right there is the pure Godly definition of risk that God wants all of His children to understand, comprehend, and live from.

Ever heard of the butterfly effect? It is to be said that a butterfly could flap its wings and cause a hurricane on the other side of the world. But aren't hurricanes bad and cause damage? Yes, they can be, but the rain could bring harvest and refresh the driest of places. What looks so terrible to us can bring God the greatest glory. We just have to be willing to take that leap of faith and actually do what is on our hearts. "But Beka, how do I know what to do?" That is an excellent question, and I have struggled with the same one day in and day out. I have been told to listen to what God is saying, and that in itself is risky because there are so many voices around us that we can listen to, which brings me to being intentional about risk. As I mentioned before, risk can be a noun or a verb. When it's used as a verb, it has to be intentional to achieve what we hope to be greatness.

Do you know of a single person who willy nilly took a risk and didn't have intention behind it? I know of several, and it hasn't turned out so great.

I am a firm believer in speaking things into existence. I recently learned that hesitation is actually the opposite of courage. It's not fear. We may have the courage to do something (risk) but are allowing hesitation to stop us, to freeze us in our steps. How do we overcome such hesitation? By being intentional and talking about it. Going out boldly in faith, proclaiming that we will be perfectly fine. Our biggest battles are our own mindsets. When our minds start to fail us and make us think we aren't going to survive, that's when the chance or risk of death/suffering becomes far more prevalent in our lives.

What risks have you taken thus far in your journey of life? Can you think of any? How about raising a kid? Falling in love? In these next several chapters, I will talk about the different risks I have taken and the outcomes of each one.

{ 2 }

Outcomes: Good or Bad

Every single risk you take in life will have some sort of outcome. It can be good or bad, and sometimes it can change in the middle or even later. I don't think there is any system as to what will bring a good or bad outcome, besides the root of your intention behind it. You, my friend, were born for adventure, so why don't you take more risks?

I believe there is a deep-rooted fear in all of us that is deeply afraid of bad outcomes. Yet, we are all made in glory, with good hearts. So why do we fear the bad so much? Maybe it's because of what we fill our minds with most of the time? Think about it. When you wake up, what is the very first thing you do? For me personally, I have a habit of catching up on social media, looking at memories, and that always brings up some sort of negative news. Others of you may get up, make coffee, and turn on the news, which is filled with negativity! Very rarely do I see positive stories. We all tend to feed on drama; what people are doing appears worse than what we are currently doing. It's all about comparison.

I also feel that we base our risks on the outcomes of what happened to other people. It's a solid motivation to learn from others, but what we learn is a key factor. We see everywhere that so and so did this and, it resulted in a great way; therefore, it must be great for me too. Ever have that thought process? I certainly have. I have even had the opposite, where I look at someone doing something far worse than me, and I am all of a sudden feeling better about myself because I seem to have a better outcome than the other person. Or I even justify my wrongdoings because I am not as bad as that person. So, why do we fall into this trap? I am still figuring that out, but I have learned that we long for great things and are just trying to achieve as much greatness as possible in our time on earth.

As I have been writing this book, there has been great animosity in our country. Racial wars, things shut down because of Covid, and the trending topic of sex trafficking. There is a great risk to all of it. Especially when it comes to sharing our thoughts and opinions on each subject. Personally, fighting the injustice of sex trafficking of children should be the thing we all want to fight right now. This statement right here is a risk to talk about because many, many others disagree with me. I have gained more enemies in the past five months because of what I stand for. I believe racism exists, sex trafficking exists, and even the Coronavirus exists and has been deadly to some people. However, I disagree with the way that everything has been handled. People are starving, have no income, have incurred more debt because of job loss, have been killed, had their life savings burned to the ground from the anger of others, are constantly fighting with each other, and the list could go on. Everything happening right now is absolutely shattering my heart. I pray that Jesus comes back soon because we desperately need Him to do just that. I have had several people get angry with me, unfriend me, cuss me out, you name it all because I stand for things that seem to go against the current trending belief. But hey, Chris-

The Greatest Risk of All

tianity is the same thing. More people than not want to believe that we are accidentally put here, having to go around blind figuring out what exactly we are here for. Despite that popular belief, I believe that Jesus came to save us all, provide a way of escape, and show us, unconditional love.

Now let me tell you, living this way, in the current status of the world and as a recovering people pleaser, is extremely difficult. I hate animosity, confrontations, and arguments more than many people seem to. I hate losing people, I can't stand to make people mad, but I love God and the things He stands for way more. Standing firm in everything that I mentioned causes a lot of bad outcomes, but they are surface-level bad. By the world's standards, they are bad. But by God's standards, they are good. He never once promised me or anybody else an easy life, as He tells us in His word.

"I have told you these things, so that in me you may have peace. In this world you will have trouble. But take heart! I have overcome the world." John 16:33

So despite all of the negative, evil things going on, I can still cling to the peace that only comes from God. I know that He knew all of this would happen, and I find the greatest comfort of all knowing that.

Just like there are bad outcomes, there are also really great outcomes. There can be surface-level great outcomes and then deep-rooted great outcomes. Most of the time, the latter ones show up later in life. However, I don't always see them right away. One primary example that comes to mind is when I talked to my friend about her contemplating an abortion. If you ever attempted to talk a friend out of this, I am sure you know exactly what I am talking about. This topic hits home for me for various reasons, but the main reason is that when I had my firstborn, Lily, I was scared to have her. I was scared of what people would say, specifically my parents, and I was scared of being a mom and having to deal with child delivery. All of which is completely normal to be scared of; after all, I am human. And because of that fear, I was highly considering an abortion. However, I was determined to take the pill and have it done naturally. I will touch more on this in a later chapter, but it haunts me from time to time even thinking about this. For the whole first year of Lily's life, I would look at her and break down crying because I felt so ashamed that I wanted to kill her. That being said, I feel like I have some personal ground to stand on when trying to convince my friends not to make that decision.

I can tell you that this conversation has happened on two different occurrences and both times were not easy at all. There was a lot of fighting, confrontation, and then I couldn't sleep for a while because I was so stressed and upset. I desperately wanted my friends to see my perspective and I put in a ton of work to the point where I had nothing left to say. The immediate outcome of both of these? BAD. I hated losing sleep or the thought of losing girlfriends that I held near and dear to my heart, but I wasn't about to give up without a fight.

The great news and great outcome of both situations are that neither of them had an abortion. How amazing is that?! Gosh, I can't tell you how thrilled I am. I have had the privilege of keeping in touch with one of them and their child. The other one, well, life happens, and we drifted apart, but I will say that she ended up messaging me a few years ago to tell me how grateful she was that I had that hard talk with her because without me, well, I should say

The Greatest Risk of All

without God. After all, it was really His doing through me that she wouldn't be celebrating her child's birthday every year. It gives me chills and a big ole smile reflecting on both of these. But man, I will tell you that was a hard journey to take on.

In other situations, it could be a great outcome initially, stay good for a while, then turn out very bad. Starting great would be more like surface-level greatness that the human eye can see. One example of this is dating someone who seems great in the beginning and turns out abusive in some fashion. This is another subject I will dive deeper into later on.

Overall, I would encourage all of you to look at outcomes in a new light. The best outcomes are when they are great on an internal or spiritual level. Because if you are a Christ-follower, those are what we will eventually be rewarded for. God wants to bless each one of us. If we live our lives doing great deeds for others with the best Godly intentions, God will reward us with endless riches. Possessions, wealth, and any other earthly gain will eventually mean nothing, so I would encourage you to start earning your rewards in Heaven from the deepest part of my heart! What a great joy it will be that day for us when we get to reflect with God on all the ways we have benefited others around us in words and actions that reflect God and His love! I don't know about you, but I can't wait.

{ 3 }

Hearing from God: How?

Have you ever questioned someone when they talk about hearing from God and how easy it seems to be for them? I have many times. Whenever someone told me to listen to God and practice hearing from Him, I was like, what in the heck do you mean? His voice isn't audible, so it can be pretty difficult, especially when louder voices surround us daily.

Something I practice daily is journaling. When I first started to hear from God, I really had to pay attention and act on what I thought God was saying. Usually, these voices were not my own, and they were random thoughts I would have. So I would proactively challenge it, write about it, and then see what the outcome could be.

I keep two journals. One of which, I write to God with a different topic each day, but it's a five-day pattern.

1. Thanksgiving - I thank Him for everything He is currently doing in my life.
2. Praise and Worship - I focus on praising all of His attributes and worshipping Him through words.

3. Request - I share with Him what is on my heart and what I think at the time He is guiding me to ask for.
4. Relationship - I discuss with Him who He is to me.
5. God's Response - this one is really fun because it gives me a chance to really sit there and write a letter from God to me.

I have kept this rhythm up for three years now, so it is really cool that I am able to flip back and see the ways God has spoken to me over the years. In fact, God has told me to write this book for about four years now, and I have started and re-started this book about five times.

The first time I started to write, it was basically a very sad sob story about how awful my life had been. I fully detailed everything in my life but from a negative viewpoint. Then I rewrote it, hoping to have a positive twist to it, but that was still awful. Then I attempted to create four different books, filled with 365 letters that I wrote to someone I thought I was in love with four years ago. I erased all of that and started a book about risk similar to what I am writing now, but I worked so hard a couple weeks ago to update my laptop, which required deleting a lot of documents, which happened to include my book. Go figure. So now I am writing about risk for a second time with a different mindset. This time is different from any other time I have tried to write. For one, I am a stay-at-home mom, while my husband works full time, so I have many chances to sit and write. And secondly, I am finally in the best position with God, with a very positive view of my story that I am able to write about it in a beautiful way to give others encouragement.

In addition to journaling, I am able to hear from God through what other people say. Not too long ago, I met with a good friend for coffee, and we discussed all the troubles I had been having lately with friendships. I felt broken and mistreated. After conversing with her, she informed me that I had abandonment issues. I was like, "holy crap, pump the breaks. Say what?" We discussed this further, and she basically put it this way; I never was physically abandoned, but I have had emotional abandonment from my parents and others I held near and dear to my heart, and it had literally screwed me up mentally for all these years. I was putting so much into my relationships, giving them my heart, and then pretty much letting them tell me my worth.

At that moment, I felt like a piece of me had shattered and finally, let in the light I had been missing all of this time. How crazy it was to hear this! I could feel God speaking to me directly through her and telling me that this was something I needed to move forward. I needed it to heal and remember exactly who I was to Him to have beautiful relationships and, more importantly, a beautiful marriage that reflects God. Shortly after our conversation, I got a tattoo on my right forearm that says, "I am worthy." Man, it has definitely been a conversation starter. I thought I got it just for me, but it has given me many opportunities to talk to people about it and give them light and encouragement.

I will also say that I have encountered people who have boldly told me, "I think God is telling you...." I wish I could insert some angry emoji here because that is the opposite of what God wants and desires for each of us. In the experiences that I have truly heard what God is saying through others to me, NEVER have, and I repeat, never started with that phrase. I firmly believe that we are

The Greatest Risk of All

God's messengers, and although He speaks through us, He often doesn't reveal that in advance so that He gets all the glory. Have you ever told someone something, and they had a similar reaction to what I did with my friend? It doesn't always necessarily go that route, but when it does, I sense in that instant that it was genuinely God. I also am completely at a standstill and reflect on everything I just said, wondering how that even came out of my mouth. It is absolutely insane but amazing at the very same time.

Another way that I practice hearing from God is by reading His Word and reading books by other Christian authors. I don't always get exactly what I need from God's Word right away; I am still practicing that one, but hearing another believer talk about different Biblical passages and their input on it, helps a lot! I love getting a new devotional each year filled with Bible verses and short devotionals about them and reading other books, especially Lysa Terkheurst. If you haven't heard of her, look her up. Her books are seriously amazing, inspiring and have helped me in many ways. I hope I get the privilege of meeting her and talking with her! That would be a dream come true for me as a writer. I need all the inspiration I possibly can get!

There are a few more ways you can hear from God, which are very amazing and creative. I am still working on all of them because I long to hear from God in every single way possible. Lord knows I absolutely need it and can't get enough! But I will stick at the ones I am successful in right now.

God speaks through dreams, through nature, through stillness, and through simple actions. I haven't really experienced God through dreams, I have had some visions, though, sometimes about positive things, but those didn't really come true. I am still working on that one. A friend recently told me about grounding, where you go enjoy nature barefooted and truly feel at one with nature. I believe this would be a positive step towards peace and hearing from God through nature. As far as stillness goes, I am not the best at being still and at rest. But when I do experience it, I am able to hear from God. This one is difficult for me because my mind races, and it's hard to really clear my mind and allow the thoughts of God to sweep in and clear out everything. The last one, simple actions, can be tough as well. I have experienced it through walking and then having a nudge of "pick up that piece of trash you saw," or "pray for this person," and the most recent one I had was to reach out to someone I don't even know and try to give her love and encouragement. She hasn't responded yet, but I definitely know it was something I needed to do because it's no longer a pressing thought in my mind, and I have peace.

If you notice, I talk about peace a lot. This is what I strive for daily. Anytime I am trying to do something in a direction that I believe God is guiding me to, I strive to have peace through it. More often than not, I feel the disruption in my life, a heavy beating of my heart until I do what God is laying on my heart. I would compare it to having anxiety. Has anyone experienced that? I do a lot, and it drives me crazy. I hate the anxious feelings that I get, but I believe they are God's way of helping me see that something needs to change or be done. So I actively long to stay calm, at peace, and do whatever it takes to calm my nerves.

Before I dive into the next chapter, I want to leave you with this. Take some time to practice hearing from God in one of the ways I mentioned. If you already have experienced hearing from

The Greatest Risk of All

Him, try a new way that you aren't super fluent in. I know that each of us has our strong method in which we hear from God, but I believe it is a goal that all of us should hear from Him in many ways. How amazing would that be? That no matter what you are doing in life, you have an opportunity to hear from Him. Children are the absolute best at it because they have no baggage that blurs the line of communication between them and God. If you have a child, ask them to draw you a picture or talk to them about their dreams. Those are two prevalent ways that God communicates through them, and it's actually very powerful! Plus, it gets them started early with practicing, and God can say things to them that will inspire us as parents daily.

{ 4 }

God's Will: What Direction do I go?

Before I get into different risks I have taken in the course of my life, I find it best to talk about God's will for each of our lives that require us to take those risks.

I am sure most of you have heard of God's will, but it can be quite difficult to comprehend sometimes. Some of us think that it would be so much easier to just get the plain, black and white layout of His will for each of our lives. But would it really, though? I personally don't think it would. Jesus followed God's will on His time here on earth, and it involved Him dying on the cross. Even He pleaded and begged with God about His will.

"My Father, if it be possible, let this cup pass from me; nevertheless, not as I will but as you will." Matthew 26:39

I don't know about you, but this verse strikes a chord with me. There have been so many times where I have tried to argue with God about Him putting me through something that makes me quite uncomfortable or something even painful, and I just want out of it. Ever been there? I can't tell you how many times I have experienced that during my 30 years on this earth, but I have. I can't even begin to imagine what Jesus was going through pain-wise when He knew God's will involved Him dying. I love that after He ques-

The Greatest Risk of All

tioned God, Jesus still said not what He would do but what God's will for His life on this earth. This is the faith I have been actively working to grow each and every day. I long to have this radical faith even in the face of death.

Even though Jesus was perfect in every way, He experienced everything we do when it comes to emotions. So as you can imagine, He felt a variety of emotions and temptations leading up to His death. Could you imagine being faced with a death sentence and not doing anything wrong at all? It is extremely difficult for me to wrap my head around it, but it's so inspiring and enlightening that Jesus went through it anyway. The beauty was, unlike us, He was fully divine and fully human, so He knew from a very young age what God's plan was for Him, who He was, and what the end result was going to be. He was put on earth to spread love, be a disciple, and then die in order to save everyone else from eternal death. However, because He was perfect, He was able to handle everything, well, perfectly. He never did any wrong things and never failed God even though He knew He was going to die. I can't comprehend that knowledge and not react negatively.

This brings me to figuring out God's will. I am so glad that God hasn't revealed absolutely everything to me from birth that was going to happen in my lifetime. I don't want to know when I am going to die, how it's going to happen, or anything like that at all. It would be so scary to know all of that, and would I really live any differently knowing that? I am honestly not promised tomorrow, ever. Every day is a gift, and I still fail each and every day through my words and actions. Some say knowledge is power, but I beg to differ with that statement, faith is power. Knowledge doesn't get you anywhere; it's what you do and who you believe in that helps you progress and move forward successfully in this lifetime.

Recently, Pastor Judd at Central Church spoke on God's will. The overall message touched on how we as believers tend to think that God's will is so unknown, so scary to the point where we question what we are doing and where we are going a lot. Or some of us don't even think it really exists and kind of just go with the flow doing what we want. And for others, we think God's will should make things easier, but the exact opposite is true. He said, "Sometimes God's will includes a wall knowing it will not make it easier. This wall can not keep you from what God has already given you." He touched on this topic because we were going through the book of Joshua when the Israelites were promised the overtake of Jericho, but God called them to march around the walls of Jericho before God would just give it to them.

When following God's will, these "walls" that each of us faces definitely make coming to the other side of God's blessings and promises so much harder, but it makes it so worth it. Conquering and overtaking each of our walls requires an immense amount of faith that God longs for each of us to have. It also requires a ton of humility. Pastor Judd mentioned, "Look up to God and look in with humility. When we are at a wall, listen to what God wants us to do as His servant." We will never get anywhere in life thinking we are in control of everything that happens to us. Sure, we can control our actions, reactions, to an extent, our emotions, and even who we surround ourselves with. All of these factors are key to helping us succeed and move forward in God's will for our lives.

The Greatest Risk of All

During this sermon, Pastor Jud gave us a bullseye view of what God's will looks like. If you're a frequent Target shopper like me, this symbol should be easy to visualize. The outer ring is God's specific will which is what we try to figure out. The middle ring is God's moral will: love mercy, and love others. And the inner circle is God's ultimate will. This is that we grow closer to Him and love Him above all else. So oftentimes, when we are going through something and trying to figure out what to do, as long as it aligns with the inner two circles, we can walk confidently hand in hand with God, waiting patiently for His blessings and seeing what the outcome of that scenario will be. But if it is completely against the inner two circles, we can be confident and have the utmost faith in God that that is not a direction we should be following, and He is trying to shut that door.

I will say that following these guidelines with the target visualization does help with a lot of decisions, but it doesn't always help lay out the map of our life. I believe there is a lot of things God is okay with and wants for us, but it's not necessarily the perfect timing for it which requires us to wait and continue to conquer the walls set before us to achieve it. This concept may sound foreign to you right now, but I hope you can have a better grasp of it like I do by the end of this book. Heck, I am still figuring things out as I go along for the ride, but because of my experience with different risks I have taken, I believe I have a lot to offer each of you as readers that can help you in your walk with God. And if you're reading this and have no relationship with God because you don't believe in Him, for whatever reason why you picked this up, I hope I can be an inspiration to you in some way, that you can experience God's love, and know that I am praying for you too.

One last thought I want to leave you with about God's will and the processes that follow it, is a thought by Lysa Terkeurst. In her book *It's Not Supposed to Be This Way*, there's a chapter called Fighting Words, and in this chapter, she discusses having different words to fight with when battling attacks from the enemy. When the enemy attacks, he means business and is trying to deter each of us from God's will and His blessings that follow. She uses an example of wine being poured into a new vessel to avoid it becoming stagnant or complacent. She then goes on to say, "to be poured into new vessels may seem uncomfortable, chaotic, and completely unfair in the moment, but it's our only hope of seeing what God wants us to see and trusting Him in it. This is what Jesus did. This is what Jesus modeled. To be like Jesus, we must become more and more saturated with Him and less saturated with our human ways of processing circumstances."

I have to tell you, reading this after hearing about a message of God's will, it was completely perfect, and that's when I realized I just had to write about it when talking about risk. Following God and His will is extremely hard, and there will be days that are completely uncomfortable, but it is completely worth it at the end when you reap all the rewards and blessings God wants to give. It requires extraordinary faith, stepping out of our comfort zone, and moving forward, even if it's just little baby steps. God's will for each of us is to never stay stagnant like wine or like water. It's to move and trust that God has a plan even when we can't see the end.

{ 5 }

Purpose: Can God use Me?

Raise your hand if you have ever had a concern about this question. Okay, now put your hands back down. Like many of you, I have also asked this question time and time again. For probably the majority of my life, I have battled with this question. But God, can you really use me after all of the mistakes I have made? The answer to any or all of the many different versions of this question is a resounding YES. God can 100,000% use you. BUT the only thing that stops us from being used by God is us. Can you believe that?

I feel that too often in this lifetime, we are told to do the right thing, stay on the path and watch God work His so-called magic in our lives, but do any of us really stick to that plan? I can tell you I have not. You see, we are all hard-wired in sin, it stinks, but that's the truth. We are born human, which means we are, in reality, born to fail. We are born broken but yet covered in grace at the same exact time. It's an amazing thing to be able to grasp that concept, but at the same time, it's a tough pill to swallow.

If you think about it, what stories do you learn from the most? Ones where everything was perfect, the person never made any mistakes, never had any turmoil, never experienced drama, or anything traumatic. Or do you learn from the difficult stories where people trudge through the literal depths of hell, experience hurt, pain, and all the emotions in between? I definitely learn from the latter. The only perfect person I have ever learned from is Jesus, but even He had an immense amount of pain and struggle, which makes His story and time here on earth so beautiful.

None of us are exactly like Jesus, so it's hard to figure out how God can possibly use each of us. But I am passionate about this. Figuring out God's will and all the risks that it may include along the way really starts with realizing our true genuine primary purpose and remembering at all times that God can use you in every single way. We just have to allow Him to do just that.

We are all taught that being "used" is bad. No one likes to be used. Not by friends, boyfriends or girlfriends, siblings, or even parents. Have you ever felt like a pawn in someone else's life? If so, you are not alone. I've been used by exes, siblings, and even by my own mother. My pain and trauma have been exemplified in words she shares with strangers to have the upper hand in an argument. She's even used a risk I took that ended in pain for her own glorification. Well, at least she tried to become the one everyone should feel sorry for. However, the point in my story is not to bash my mom and the pain she has caused me in my life. The point I am trying to make is that, for one, I am sure I am guilty of it too. Secondly, the main reason of all is that God uses us for His glory, His kingdom, and we can rest knowing all of the ways He uses us is for good.

I think that is a big battle for the majority of us. We are so used to people using our pain or even causing us pain for their benefit and their own satisfaction that it's extremely hard to believe that someone much greater than the universe can use everything we go

The Greatest Risk of All

through for good and for His ultimate glory. But friends, it's so true that He does. We cannot possibly know God's will or trust that the risks we take can be good without knowing that ultimately, our whole lives are very much created to tell the love of God, His good work, and to rebuild His kingdom. So no, it's not a question of "can He use us," but it's merely a question of "He wants to use us, we get to be used, so will we let Him?" To think about how the God of the whole universe wants a relationship with us, and we actually get to play a part in His bigger plan is completely mind-blowing! It's so earth-shattering, and it's a humbling experience once you can grasp it.

Have you ever felt pride and confidence once you've completed a project for school or work, and the outcome was an A+ all around for everyone, made your co-workers or boss look good, and it resulted in extra credit or even a promotion? I sure have experienced that, and man, does it feel good. It feels good because, at that moment, we see the shining looks on everyone's faces, we see the immediate results, the pats on our backs, the glory we worked so hard to achieve. And have you ever seen that experience come crumbling down in an instant, not mattering anymore, the drama, the chaos, someone got hurt and caused a scene? Boy, can that list of turmoil continue and have quite the snowball effect. That, I have also experienced. How quickly this life and all that we do in it can go from soaring the highest of highs to trudging through the lowest of lows in an instant. Poof, all that hard work suddenly dissipates, and we question what was that even for? So we get discouraged, we question everything we are currently doing. I. CAN. RELATE. It's awful and heart-wrenching. It's happened way too many times than I can count and quite possibly bear.

So that circles me back to "God, you put me through this, can You really use me, when I have failed at every other responsibility?" Yes, yes, and a thousand times, yes! Just like we have an almighty God, who wants to use us for His glory, and everything I have already mentioned, there is also an enemy that walks among us who wants to make us feel like everything we do is an incomplete mission, a failed attempt, that we aren't good enough or equipped enough. Thankfully, we have what's called the armor of God (Ephesians 6:11) to combat all of these lies. To hold onto the very truth that God gives us. He doesn't call those who are equipped, who have it all together, He equips the ones He calls - (1 Corinthians 1:27-29)

You, my friend, are being called by Him to take these risks, to be used by Him. The ultimate purpose of all of us is to show God's love, and build His kingdom, and then spend eternity with Him in Heaven. But, because we are made differently in unique ways with various gifts, we all have different specific purposes that give us meaning for our lives and things to do, so we aren't just running around aimlessly. Which I tend to do when I am not listening. I can tell you that you will take much more risks once you figure out that you have a purpose for good, how to hear from God, and figure out the beauty of following His will for your life. Realizing that you matter and that God chose you and called you for very specific reasons. How do we find those out? By taking risks. We will never know what we are supposed to do sitting on the couch watching Netflix every day or staying stagnant. Taking risks is exhilarating, and ultimately, it's comforting knowing that God will always have your back and is guiding you through everything.

The risks I have taken that I will discuss in the next several chapters definitely aren't meant for everyone. I have a different

The Greatest Risk of All

personality than a lot of you. My passions, dreams, desires, and sense of adventure are different. I hate staying at home most days, so forcing myself to sit and write with no distractions can be quite the challenge, but I am determined and firmly believe this is part of my purpose here in this life. Not to explain how terrible my life has been, not even to convince you to do some of the crazy things I have done, but to hopefully encourage some of you to break out of your shell, take those risks you have been afraid to take, and ultimately take a risk on God, and see what He can do. Are you jumping out of your seat yet? If not, hopefully, you will by the time you reach the end of the story God has blessed me with. So sit back, and hang on tight; this ride is about to get a bit bumpy.

Risk #1: High School

Oh boy, where do I even begin? High school has got to be one of the most challenging times for teenagers. It's a time when we are all still attempting to figure out who we are, yet it's also a time to thrive, meet people, experience all sorts of "firsts." First job, first prom-type setting, first significant other, getting a license, you name it.

My high school experience was different than the majority, I would say because I went to a Christian school that was small and affiliated with the church my family and I attended. So I basically saw the same community of people five to six days a week, which was pretty awesome. I started that school when I was in Kindergarten. When I was about to begin my Junior year, my little sister and brother transferred out of our school to a nearby public school since they weren't having such a great experience. Well, just like them, I also had the opportunity to change schools, but I turned it down because there was no way I was about to change schools when I only had two more years to go. And frankly, I wanted to stick around the same group of people I had already been doing life with. I gained some of the best friends through my high school days and unfortunately lost some of them several years later, but we will get to that.

The Greatest Risk of All

My sophomore year, I got my braces off and got my driver's license too. Then the beginning of my junior year, I started a new job at a local movie theatre. This started my journey of significant risks I have taken.

Most of my classmates and friends at the time weren't really working like I was, or if they did maybe, they weren't working as much. Because I got my first "big girl" job at the theatre, it required a lot of long hours, nights, and boy; I got exhausted pretty quick. I also started to become, let's say, "of the world" during this job. Being at a Christian school and baptist church most of my life, I never really had to establish good grounds to stand on when it came to my faith. Sure I believed in God, went to church, and was that "good girl" that everyone saw because I could pretty much live off of everyone else's faith. Everyone else seemed to believe and do the right things, but boy was I naive.

Once I started working and getting to know my coworkers, the more I became involved with them, pressured by them, and started to become like them as well. I quickly went from being a good Christian girl to someone who wasn't the greatest representation of God and His love. This started my downward spiral into many risks that had some pretty bad outcomes along the way.

I never cussed growing up, and I remember being pressured to say the baddest word of them all, that's right, folks, the F word. I got pressured and pressured to say it, and then I started to cuss a lot more around these people. I felt somewhat free, and I felt like I needed to be liked and included. I started to hang out with them more because I went from outcast to in-crowd; wanted and valued with them. I had a lot of very fun Friday nights with them. After work, we would usually go bowling or to the park, and during the summer, we would go swimming at all hours of the night. During this time, I became infatuated with some of the boys I worked with.

Fast forward a year and a half, and soon it was time for my senior prom, which fell on the 18th of that month and happened to be my 18th birthday. So it was my golden birthday, a pretty dang special day if I do say so myself. Leading up to this point, I had denied myself feeling any particular way for any of these guys, or at least I very much tried to because they weren't saved. And I was taught growing up that I needed to date another believer. Now that I am 30 and married, I understand why. But the 17 going on 18-year-old Beka wanted to make excuses or missionary date. Drag them to church, pray for them; you know the whole shebang to have what I felt deep down in my heart wasn't right.

Any-who, since it was my senior year, birthday, and senior prom all in one, I knew I had to have the perfect date. What better date than my best guy friend at the time, who happened to be in a relationship at that moment. But some part of me longed so badly for them to break up, and shortly after, that wish of mine was granted. They had just broken up, and I remember him stopping me in the hallway, asking me to go to prom with him, and I was excited beyond belief. I just couldn't even believe it! I mean, come on, you guys, surely the 18-year-old you is rejoicing with me at this moment. Unfortunately, this excitement was definitely a risk because, sure enough, that dream got crushed as quickly as it happened.

The Greatest Risk of All

Sometime between the remaining of the school day, getting home, and talking to my best friends about this momentous occasion, they got back together! That's right, my very best guy friend, someone I was crushing on hard at the time, got back together with his ex the same day I got asked to prom by him. Of course, when I found this out, I was crushed. But yet he was still willing to take me to prom as a fulfillment of his promise to me, and I was all for it, until a few days later.

After all of this went down, the next couple of days at school were pretty terrible. I remember being approached by her friends, saying how awful I was for still considering going with him to prom. I kept being told, "well, wouldn't you want to go with your boyfriend to your senior prom too?" I could answer that with a firm, yes, but I wasn't able to relate completely, and after all, he did ask me, was still willing to take me, and it wasn't my fault they broke up and got back together in the first place. But, man, I gotta say, writing about this moment and reflecting on it, it really takes me back and gives me not-so-great feelings, ugh. But I will move forward in my story, regardless.

Ah yes, the days after were very miserable and not fun in the least. I felt attacked, and I felt like a knife got shoved through my gut. I felt betrayed, and a lot of other negative feelings were evolving one by one. Then finally, one night when I felt like I couldn't bear it any longer, I had a long talk with one of my best friends, and she encouraged me to say no to him because he wasn't going to deny me and to find someone else to go with. Boy, was I crushed. This royally sucked. So I called him, he fought with me and still insisted anyway, so of course, I told my friend everything that was said. Her comment was, "no, Beka, you are flat out going to have to tell him no, and not ask, and be stern about it. It's the right thing to do."

Ever been in a position like this? Why does doing the right thing hurt so bad? It's really difficult, and this is all a part of risk, and I am sure if you haven't experienced it yet, you will at some point.

What felt like hours later, I finally did what she advised me to do, but this time it was over text because I was not about to have another phone conversation with him. Things got even worse, because as fate would have it, his mom checked his phone every evening, and sure enough, she saw my text to him. I can't exactly recall what I had sent, but I do remember saying something about how he hurt me and that I was very upset over it, but I didn't want to stand in his way.

Needless to say, all of those bad days at school I thought I already had, snowballed into a bigger disaster because his mom denied him going to senior prom because of what I did, which then led to his girlfriend not wanting to attend anymore, so she and all of her friends were pretty upset, to say the least. For days following these events, I remember that's all anyone could talk about, or so it seemed. I was asked to speak with his mom about it, but I remember coming to the conclusion that there was nothing I could do about it really because it was up to his mom.

Looking back on these events, I realized it was definitely a risk I took to speak my mind, be honest, and do the right thing. Even though the outcome was unpleasant for some people, I believe that because of me taking that risk of doing the right thing, God ended up protecting me, protecting my evening away from drama and the

The Greatest Risk of All

people who created harm and hurt for me. I didn't see it at the time, but I definitely do now.

I am sure at this point, some of those who have known me since my high school and college days, otherwise known as my "rebellion and scandalous days," are probably rolling their eyes. I can imagine that some of them picked up this book to get to know some of the deep dark secrets that have been hidden from them, and don't worry, I am getting there for sure, but I felt right in my heart to start where it all began so be patient please, and let me continue.

Do you recall towards the beginning of this chapter when I mentioned that I became infatuated with some of the guys I worked with? Well, there was one specific guy that I know I tended to annoy sometimes because I just always wanted to talk to him. In order to protect his identity, I will call him Winston. Well, you see Winston, was definitely extraordinary because literally, all the girls that we worked with or became friends with in our circle all had a thing for him at some time or another. He was attractive, outgoing, funny, witty, kind, protective. He was very much dreamy in all of our eyes, and he was actually the one I was able to take as my date to senior prom. Which was extremely fun but turned out to be a disaster later on, but we will get to that.

Leading up to this very special day, my parents had been in cahoots with my very best friends, who helped my parents pull off the ultimate surprise for my birthday. They had planned a surprise party, which was also the after-prom party, and had booked a limo for my friends and me to go to this party. And boy was I surprised!

I am definitely blonde, as my mom would say, "to the roots." Meaning I don't have to be blonde on the outside, but my brain definitely has a lot of blonde moments. I say stupid things sometimes, and make people laugh. I have grown to adapt to it and not mind, since making people laugh is a great quality to have. Well, since I am so very blonde, this whole surprise completely snuck past me. My friends had asked to borrow my phone to get numbers of people to let them know what was going on, and I remember them going to the school office one day without me, and they kept so many secrets. I was pretty upset by this because I genuinely had no clue what was going on.

When the limo came to pick us all up, I even saw the driver holding a sign that said my name on it, and I was like, "wow, that Beka girl is really lucky her parents got her a limo. Jenny, where is your dad with the van to pick us up?" Of course, everyone laughed and screamed, "Beka, this is for you!" I was seriously blown away.

During this whole time, I could tell that my date was taking a special liking to one of my best friends. Can you imagine the pain of that? They were connecting in ways far beyond I imagined, and spoiler alert, they are married now. Turns out she had gotten his number, and they were talking very frequently. Needless to say, this caused some major drama later on.

A month after this big event, it was time for our Senior trip. Every year, the seniors at our school got to go to Florida since our school was so small. My class had 49 people in it. So we went to Florida, like all of the classes before us, and I gotta say, my best friends and I fought a lot. The one that connected with my prom date talked to him pretty much our whole trip, and I was jealous and not very happy. I felt left out, and I was like, I am the reason

The Greatest Risk of All

you two met, so why am I left out? My jealousy got the better of me, and of course, I talked to her a lot about it which made for a pretty rough time.

Shortly after, it was time to graduate, go to college, and experience some of our last summers together. I thought I was fully prepared for the risk of college and even growing apart, but I really wasn't.

Reflecting on some of my issues in high school, especially there at the end, I wish I could take some of what I said back. I wish I could have ended things smoother than I did, not get jealous, remember that guy wasn't good for me anyway, see red flags, and keep my mouth shut even when I was in pain. But the risk of being open, vulnerable, and honest with how I was feeling helped me see the true colors of people and helped me see that this world wasn't the bubble I grew up in.

I know I ruined friendships, and I deeply miss them too. In the next several chapters, you'll see how all of this panned out with the pain it has caused me and mistakes that were made years later because of those risks I took. Would I take them back if I could? It would certainly be tempting, but I believe all of those issues helped shape me in the years following, being vocal, vulnerable, and not letting my heart get stomped on like I did prior.

The risks ended in some pain, lonely nights, but over time, it ended up for the better, and I definitely see the beauty from it.

{ 7 }

Risk #2: College

Who remembers gearing up for their first day of college? Usually, the summer between graduating high school and heading to college is super fun and exciting, getting things for your dorm, etcetera. Well, that wasn't the case for me.

By the time graduation rolled around, I was that graduate that was undecided on a college. I felt pretty awful that I had no idea what I was going to do. I am sure I am not the only one who has gone through this, but I am a planner. I love to plan, stay ahead, but ironically I am also a procrastinator. College was different, though; I just wanted a plan on what I was going to do so I could seriously stop stressing!

Sure enough, just like my mother always did, she helped me. We decided that I would go away for college to Liberty University in Virginia. She had bought me dorm room supplies, even a Liberty hoodie. But I was deep down terrified to leave home and my friends from work and our neighborhood. I wanted so badly to go away and get the full-blown college experience that everyone seems to get, but I was also very much dreading the thought of leaving people I had loved to do life with as of late.

The Greatest Risk of All

Usually, when my mom and I decided things (mainly my mom decided, then I would agree), she would often change her mind. I really should have seen this time as no different, but I didn't. So a few weeks later, after college prepping, she had decided for me that I was going to go to our local college NKU. It was a fifteen-minute drive from home, plus I could still work at the theatre, which was also close by, live at home, and save tons of money. Which honestly was a blessing in the end for me and student loans since I didn't apply for any scholarships, but this easy and cheap way out had its fair share of risks and regrets.

August 2008 was when I started college. I had applied, got accepted, and said goodbye to some of my closest friends in high school as we all went our separate ways. Then the very first week of classes, I got struck with the news of my grandpa dying. Before this moment, I hadn't lost anyone close to me, so this was a big deal for me. The only thing that had tragically impacted my life before this was when my brother was struggling and told my parents that he didn't believe in God anymore. I will get back to this in a minute, though.

Since I didn't really prep for college like a lot of people had, I just signed up for classes, not knowing what they were going to be like or the professors. This turned around to bite me in the butt because after my grandpa died, I had to fly out to South Carolina for his funeral, and that required time off from class the very first week or so of classes. Needless to say, some of my professors were not the most understanding.

One, in particular, said I had a quiz that week, and there were no makeup quizzes, and I wasn't going to be there for it, so I literally started that class with a D. So I dropped it as soon as I could because that didn't make sense to me.

Before I continue with that, let me bounce back to my brother. He was a chaplain in high school, and I always looked up to him for years and very much admired his faith. I remember him looking at things on the computer that didn't seem right to me, and I got yelled at. My parents talked to him about it, and that's when he told them he didn't believe in God anymore. He's been an atheist ever since.

For a small-town, sheltered, Christian girl, this was earth-shattering to me. I had never experienced quite a pain like this, and then I went and got a heart on my foot as my first tattoo as a reminder that God always loves me, even when my world was shattering.

After all the chaos with my grandpa dying and figuring out things with classes, we came home, and I was still very much depressed. It was hard enough to deal with my feelings; in addition, my mom woke up and cried every day, so I began to seek comfort elsewhere.

Remember those friends from work I grew to love so much? Well, one of them, in particular, kept trying to get with me sexually. I considered him a best friend of mine, we hung out a lot, and I gotta say it was nice to feel wanted for a change. I was a virgin, and he knew that, and of course, while I was going through healing from my grandpa, he told me sex with him would make me feel better.

The Greatest Risk of All

Boy, was I naive. I never had the sex talk growing up, and even in health class as a freshman, I had no idea what a condom was. I was made fun of for years for that, but I was extremely innocent, which wasn't my fault. I never felt I needed to research anything about it; I was a very content little girl. And some boy just swooped in and took advantage of that.

I remember the day like it was yesterday. He took forever to persuade me. I can't tell you how many times I chickened out, but then I finally caved. It was trying to heal a broken heart, so it was worth it to me. I didn't know how else to deal with it.

It wasn't magical, and it was honestly something that I wish I could get out of my head, so talking about it with a bunch of people I don't know is a pretty big deal for me. It's something I am not proud of, but it is part of my journey that got me to where I am with God today, so I am willing to take this leap and talk about it.

The biggest regret I have about it was that it happened the night before his girlfriend's birthday. That's right, he was a player and didn't even care. He wanted to cheat on everyone, and I honestly didn't care at the time either. After all, I felt wanted, I was single, and I was hurting. Little did I know how fast things would catch up with me.

Fast forward about a year, and I had grown into skipping classes with my best guy friends, the one I just mentioned and another I just enjoyed being around. I would take their notes and skip class. I would also buy food and cigarette for them; you name it. I was their scapegoat. I felt like I was so wanted, and in actuality, I was being used by them 24/7, but I was too naive to actually see it, and to be honest, I didn't understand love and appreciation.

During all of this, I was still working at the movie theatre. There was one night when I had gotten into a big fight with the guy that I had given my virginity to, and I found myself at the theatre trying not to be depressed.

This particular night, a guy from the hotel next door also showed up at the theater to watch a couple of movies and also hit on my co-worker that I was hanging out with. He ended up sticking around and watching movies until she got off work, then asked her to come to the hotel and go swimming. She actually told him yes, and I was like, "hello!! Why are you going? You don't even know him?" She told me that she was going no matter what, so I could either go with her or not; it was up to me. Of course, I wanted to protect my friend, so I tagged along.

I conveniently had a bikini in my truck because I had recently gone swimming at the fitness club that my family belonged to, and I never took it out of my car. So, I was ready and able to go swimming at the hotel this night.

Our assistant manager at the time told us to be careful. I remember texting her when we got over there that the two of them had started to make out and were all over each other. I ended up sitting out of the pool, uncomfortable and pretty upset about fighting with my friends as well.

Shortly after, the girl's mom showed up at the theatre looking for her, so our manager texted me and told me so I could let her

The Greatest Risk of All

know. The girl left, and like a naive girl, I stayed. I thought the guy was interested in my friend, so why would he want anything to do with me? Boy, was I wrong. After a lot of persuasion and time spent alone, he convinced me to have sex with him.

Let me pause right now, and let you re-read that, especially you ladies. HE HAD TO PERSUADE ME AND CONVINCE ME. Guys, this is RAPE. But I had no clue! I felt like a total slut, and I remember going home just feeling all kinds of messed up. I still feel sort of messed up about this, so going into detail about it makes me utterly sick to my stomach. So I will save you the extreme details about how it all transpired, but man. I genuinely had no idea what in the heck had just happened to me.

It wasn't until about a week later that I was chatting with another girlfriend about this "slutty" event. I was like, "I met this guy the other week, and I said no about 30 times when he had asked me to have sex with him, but I caved; I am such a slut." She immediately was like, "Woah! This is rape, Beka." You need to report this. (I did, but I waited too long, so it was too late).

It took me forever to tell my parents about this. I told everyone I could before I said anything to them because I feared them blaming me. In fact, my mom did tell me, "I would have rather drowned than lose my virginity."

After I told my parents, is when I finally went to the cops about it. Because I waited so long, they couldn't prove anything, and it was deemed consensual.

Both of these statements from my mom and the cop made me start to think all of this was actually my fault and I was just some crazy person. It wasn't until I had gone out with my best friend to go hookah, and then the guy ended up calling me because my co-worker friend had his number and called him and accused him of raping me. When he called me, he was crying, and I found out he was married. He told me how scared and apologetic he was, and I really struggled with forgiving him and reporting him.

It wasn't until I had gone to my guidance counselor and talked with her, and she said, "Beka, you are able to forgive him, but that doesn't mean you can't report him too because what he did was wrong, and we need to make sure that he doesn't do to other girls what he did to you." I was very thankful she said that because it helped me be content with forgiving him and continuing the investigation of him as well. Unfortunately, he was never found because he fled the state and switched his phone number.

After all of this, I really began to question who I was and what my purpose was. I couldn't even tell you how much pain I was battling each and every day.

I also began to sleep with those two best guy friends of mine a lot more because anytime they asked me, something triggered inside of me that made me want to say yes since I actually had a choice in the matter.

The path I was spiraling down got faster and faster. Because I was spiraling down, one of my best friends from high school, the one who is now married to the guy I took to prom, actually sat me down during this time and told me how disappointed she was in

The Greatest Risk of All

me. She began to judge me for all things I told my mom I wouldn't do, like get my nose pierced, get tattoos, almost dating a guy from high school, and she, of course, didn't like how close I was with my theatre friends. It got to the point where she told me I wasn't Christian enough for her anymore.

Before I knew it, I was even more depressed. I had just lost one of my best friends, and I was flunking out of college. I was told to take a semester off to see what I actually wanted to do with my life and see if college was even for me. Then once I decided to go back, I had to write an appeal letter to my university to let them know I was serious. I changed my major for the third time and made a goal to finish in two and a half years. I felt like such a bum during my time off while everyone continued in their life journey that I was desperate to get done with my degree.

After I had this plan made, got my butt back in gear, started back in school, as fate would have it, I was eleven days late on my period.

Risk #3 Lilianna Faith

My heart began to race with emotion as I waited to see the result of that digital result on the pregnancy test I had just taken. My eyes began to well up with tears as I sat there and waited for what seemed to be the longest minute of my life. I had always been scared to have kids because the whole idea of childbirth scared everything out of me. I never dreamed of being pregnant, let alone being pregnant without being married to the father.

Leading up to this point, I had traveled a lot that summer prior to starting back in school, and I felt incredibly stressed because of everything so when I was eleven days late on my period I was like "no biggie, I have traveled and I am stressed so that's why!"

I remember being asked if I had sex recently, and I was like well yes, but that doesn't matter, we were careful. My friend was like evidently not careful enough. You just might be pregnant. I of course scoffed at her in plain denial like she didn't even have a clue what she was talking about.

It wasn't until I was with another friend the next day still kind of panicking and she had asked me if I wanted a pregnancy test be-

The Greatest Risk of All

cause she had one. I said sure, why the heck not, it will most likely be negative anyway.

This test was not negative. The tears that I was fighting to hold back this entire time began to flood out as I just sat there in despair not having a clue of what to do. My friend called a clinic for me, and we drove to the clinic there on campus and got another pregnancy test. Once again, it was positive so we discussed some options. I was thoroughly against abortion up until this point. I was so devastated and figured I couldn't handle this, so the best way out was to go as if it never even happened. Fortunately, this was a Friday evening and there was absolutely no way I could get that pill that seemed to be so natural to go ahead and end this, so I had to take the weekend to think about it even though I wasn't happy with that.

I left there feeling incredibly depressed and not wanting to be alone, so I called one of the two guys who could possibly be the father, and I hung out with him. We went and saw a movie, and I remember passing by some of our co-workers who had asked me what was wrong, I told them, including about my plan come Monday. I thank God every day for those two women. God used them to jump-start the process of radically changing my life. They weren't the only two who had gotten ahold of me this particular weekend to tell me what I would actually be doing if I were thinking rationally.

I finally walked in to watch the movie, and in between movies the guy and I had gone outside so he could smoke. He kept asking me what was wrong, and after I finally told him he said "It's the other guy's, thank God we used protection," and then high-fived me. I could not believe my eyes and ears.

During the remainder of this weekend, I told the other guy. He was with his girlfriend that weekend so he couldn't talk about it until later. I called several other girlfriends who I had gone to high school with to talk through this, and they also encouraged me to keep it. The original guy I had told however was willing and wanting to drive me to have an abortion and pay for it too. Thankfully after a lot of talking and people praying, when Monday rolled around, I just couldn't do it.

I will admit during the next twelve weeks, I was nauseous all of the time, and I honestly prayed for an abortion. I couldn't stand the thought of telling my parents. After all, they didn't take the news of my rape so well, I couldn't imagine what this time would be like. Let alone, I couldn't bear the thought of telling them "by the way I don't know who the dad is either." So I prayed and hoped for a miscarriage.

I also began to seek help from a doctor. I had tried to go through Planned Parenthood because I didn't want to go through my gynecologist until my parents knew since it would be on their insurance, but Planned Parenthood will not help women unless they are planning on getting an abortion. So I began to do other research and found the New Hope Center which is really an organization that helps pregnant women figure out the best solution that truly benefits them and their babies.

I was able to get another pregnancy test there, and also had my first ultrasound too. What a blessing they were to me!

The Greatest Risk of All

During my first ultrasound, I found out that my child was due on April 18th, my birthday. I sat there and just bawled while my friend said "happy birthday, Beka!" I was not ready for this at all. So I began to pursue adoption with the help of this center.

Weeks passed by and it was finally time to tell my parents. I waited until after twelve weeks just in case I had a miscarriage, but thankfully God did not grant me that wish.

The day I decided to tell them, I had to work pretty early, so I invited my best friends from high school over at eight in the morning, and had them stand there with me in my room while I sat my parents down and told them I was having a baby. The look of disappointment flooded their faces, and all I could hear them say was "who's the dad." I blurted out the very first name I could think of, the name of the guy I thought was the dad. I told them he didn't want to be involved, and I was already pursuing a plan for adoption. My mom was very much okay with the idea because I was informed by her many times that since I was working and in school full time, she couldn't think of being a stay-at-home grandma. however, dad very much grieved this idea.

After this conversation which seemed to take forever, I left to go to work in tears, and I finally told my manager about it too. Everyone figured out pretty quickly who the dad most likely was, after all, we all worked with them. Some of them knew for sure, some guessed, and some didn't know that I wasn't sure about who it was either, they just knew who I was prone to hang out with.

For a while, it was my dirty little secret. I dealt with the pregnancy without either man wanting to be involved. I was lonely, depressed, and tried to make the best of it I could. I began really dedicating time to finding a family for my child, and my parents decided to become involved in the family interviewing process as well. This made for a very tough situation because they had their own ideas and wants, and I had mine, so it was very hard to agree on a family together.

After many failed attempts of finding a family, about two weeks prior to my delivery I met up with a family through a mutual friend. My parents and I fell in love with them and realized they were the ones. We hung out several times, discussed all the plans we agreed on for open adoption. To us, it was perfect.

Remember how my first due date was projected as my birthday? Well when I went to the gynecologist for the first time, they told me my due date was April 9th. When April 10th rolled around I asked to be induced, and they said they didn't do that until I was late, but I told them that they kept telling me my due date was the 9th so I was late now. They went and scattered through the paperwork, then came back and said "no your due date is April 18th."

Now let me tell you, being 40 weeks pregnant, feeling ready to pop, this was not the best news. It meant I had to go one more week of pregnancy. I had already found the adoptive family and I WAS READY.

All week long after that, I had anxiously awaited to have my baby. I was so tired of being pregnant, and I just wanted to do this already.

The Greatest Risk of All

April 18th finally rolled around, and I decided to finally go to sleep at midnight. Sure enough, 45 minutes later I woke up feeling pain. I had no clue what was going on, all I knew was I couldn't sleep so I decided to get out of bed at about 6 am, and take a shower. My mom was substitute teaching at the time and had asked me if I was okay. I told her that I was having pain, and might be in labor, but I wasn't sure. So she called into the school, well at least she tried but the offices weren't open yet, so she drove out there to let them know she needed the day off. When she came home we just watch movies while she counted my contractions and the time between each one.

When it was 8 am, I called the doctor and let them know what was going on, and they told me not to come in until my contractions began to be longer and more frequent. Around 3 pm that afternoon we packed up and left to head to the hospital. I let the adopting family know, and they eventually met me there.

The doctor put me on the Pitocin drip which was supposed to help me speed up dilation, but it ended up taking me a long 13 hours to only get up to 7cm, so at 7:01 am the next morning, I had a C-section, which I pretty much planned for anyway since my mom had c-sections for all of my siblings and myself.

I remember after my surgery, the adopting mom got to hold Lily for the first time as I lay there in pain. A lot of my friends came in to meet her, and see me. I was feeling miserable and sleeping a ton. It wasn't until the next day that I finally got to meet my daughter. She was doing so well.

I remember taking a picture in the lobby holding her, along with the adopting parents, and then she left with them. I can't even begin to express the emotional pain I felt that day. I knew I was doing the right thing for her, but man, watching my baby girl leave with a family that wasn't mine, was extremely devastating.

A few weeks passed by, and I was back on campus taking my finals for my spring semester classes trying to wrap things up before my summer classes started in another week or so. I technically wasn't supposed to drive just yet, but I knew there was no way I was going to try to take new classes and take finals for my previous ones simultaneously, so I bit the bullet and did what I could do.

A week later, I was on campus starting my summer class. At this point, I had signed the paperwork I needed to for the adoption, and the guy was just now getting his part done. I remember in the middle of this class, I received a phone call from the mom who adopted Lily. I was seriously freaking out thinking they didn't love her and didn't want her anymore. Up to this point I had gone over there a couple of times with my parents to hang out with her, hold her, and I was even involved in a couple of pictures of her as well, which was cool. We had really grown to love this family and I was so afraid of anything messing it up, I was so scared to be a mom.

It's really funny how our brain musters up some of the worst-case scenarios that actually don't even happen. This phone call was actually something even more devastating than what I was thinking about.

The Greatest Risk of All

Remember that dirty little secret I had mentioned prior? Well, she told me that when the guy went to sign over his rights with a lawyer, the lawyer had asked him if he was sure he was the dad, and his response was "there is this other guy, but I am probably it." Because of that, I was invited to dinner with her and our mutual friend.

She came to this dinner wearing a new necklace she had received for mothers day, resembling her three boys, and now Lily. I remember staring at this necklace and thinking about what was going to happen. She proceeded to tell me that all of this openness my family and I had agreed on with her was now changed to my whole family only being able to see Lily once a month for an hour and a half. I began to bawl my eyes out, and she didn't seem to understand why. I left that dinner absolutely devastated questioning everything God was doing.

When I went home, I had told my mom everything that had just occurred, and I went to bed crying that night as if Lily had just died.

The next day, my parents and I talked some more and we had agreed that I needed to get her back. Although I had signed my rights over already, I had twenty-one days to change my mind from the day I signed. All of this transpired when I had ten days left, so I made the necessary phone calls to cancel the adoption and get my baby back.

Mother's Day had come and gone, and the very next day I had to go to the doctor for my post-delivery checkup, and I received a phone call letting me know our mutual friend could not make it that day, so I was on my own meeting the father outside of Olive Garden and took Lily home. I remember him asking me if I was ready to take this on, and at the time, I was super hesitant, but I assured him I knew what I was doing.

I got her home that day, and my family was all very excited to have her home, and I was full-on ready to take everything on with help. Well, at least I thought I was fully prepared. Little did I know what challenges God was going to bring to my doorstep shortly after.

{ 9 }

Risk #4: I Have Had Enough!

I would say the first part of my life was full of being walked on, taken advantage of, and being manipulated, so once I got my daughter back, I was seriously ready to go and stand up for myself and not let anyone take advantage of me any longer.

After I had her for about six months, I finally reached out to the guy who I thought was her dad, let's call him Kain. I began to tell him I needed help and that I thought his parents should know. He responded in anger and said he was about to propose to the girl he was dating and he wasn't about to let me ruin his life like that. So he demanded a paternity test. I agreed and told him I wasn't going to pay for it.

In the meantime, he had reached out to the other guy, let's call him Rhett, who contacted me asking if we could talk. I met up with Rhett, and he stood there, cried, and questioned what I would do if he ended up being the father. I told him I couldn't even think about that because somewhere in my heart, even though he had taken advantage of my emotions, I felt the need to protect him.

After we all got swabbed, I anxiously awaited the results.

Soon enough, I got a text message from the Rhett, saying that Kain wasn't the father. My heart sank. How was I about to face this new problem? I instantly called the clinic that did our testing and asked for clarification, and sure enough, Kain wasn't the dad, Rhett was.

In despair, I reached out to Kain and asked for forgiveness, and desperately tried to mend our friendship. He didn't want anything to do with me unless I paid him the $250 he just spent.

Something I do want to note about Kain, was that when he was using me as his friend with benefits, and I told him I had gotten raped. He belittled me, had called me a slut, and said that I needed to get my test results back before he could be friends with me again. So why did I want a friendship with him so bad? And neither he nor the Rhett showed up at the hospital after I had Lily. They couldn't stand to be there to be looked at as the possible dad.

Once we found out the results, I met with the guy who actually was the dad, for a second time, and we discussed details. Rhett cried again, questioned me, and then told me he was going to be there for me as a friend and pay me $100 a month.

For a while I was okay with this. We hung out, talked every day, and he paid me as he agreed. This went on for about five months or so until I started dating a guy he worked with. I was accused of treating him differently, acting differently. My breaking point started when I called his girlfriend, let's call her Luna, at the time and told her the truth of Lily's existence. That was not a fun conversation. I don't know why girls have it in their head to solely blame the girl, and not even take into consideration that their guy is at

The Greatest Risk of All

fault too. But I still took the blame I would allot myself to take, and everything else I tried to ignore.

That following weekend, Rhett went to go visit Luna, my parents were gone, and I of course worked a ton and had a loads of homework on top of it. When he was with her on the weekends, Rhett would text me until he was there, and then text me the following Sunday evening when he was on his way back. That particular conversation on his way back was not fun. He told me what a rough weekend it was for him because of what I had told Luna. However, because of the crazy stressful weekend I had just had, I wasn't super empathetic and let him know how I was feeling.

I found out years later, that he had informed her that weekend that I had raped him, which wasn't extremely pleased to find out.

Months after this encounter, he told me that he could only afford to give me $50 a month. Shortly after he said that I saw on social media that they had taken a trip to Chicago. I was so angry that I told him I was done being friends with him because I couldn't stand the thought of being friends with anyone who didn't want a relationship with my daughter, let alone her biological dad. I also decided to file for child support, and then wrote his parents a letter that included pictures of her to let them know they were grandparents.

I had told Luna that I would hope that she would be understanding and encourage him to be in Lily's life, and also encourage him to tell his parents so they could meet her as well. All she did was accuse me of was wanting money or being selfish, which wasn't the case at all.

Months went by, and I finally started receiving the child support that we needed, but I still hadn't heard from his parents. He tried to text me a few times, but I would always ignore him.

It took just shy of a year of Rhett paying child support to decide he wanted to be in Lily's life. I will never forget in October 2014. I was out to lunch with a friend, and he texted me. I was so anxious I couldn't read it so I had her read it for me instead and give me the cliff notes.

She read it and informed me that Rhett was saying he felt he needed to be involved and would like to meet Lily. I gave him a chance, met up with him, and we decided to slowly ease him into this.

It started with him seeing her every Saturday along with me. During this time he had broken up with Luna. He jumped into a new relationship with a girl that he started to cheat on Luna with. I wasn't too fond of this relationship especially because I had feelings for him, and because she all of a sudden wanted to meet Lily and spend time with all of us. I didn't have the nicest things to say about that, and certainly wasn't allowing it to happen either.

Their relationship lasted for about a month before he asked me to sleep with him again. I told him no and he was in utter shock I could even do that. He asked me "what changed?" I simply said, "I changed, and I am not going to do this." They ended up breaking up and a couple of weeks later he and I started to date. This was the first time for us, and to say I was thrilled was an understatement. I had felt God had finally answered my long-awaited prayers, and

The Greatest Risk of All

I couldn't contain my excitement about it. But fortunately for me, God slammed this door in my face pretty quickly.

At the time, I was working at a bank, and I worked with this girl who was best friends with his most current ex girlfriend's best friend. My coworker ended up telling me he cheated on me. I couldn't believe it, and when I asked him about it, he of course denied it, and I actually believed him.

Now ladies, if some guy has a history of cheating and lying, DO NOT BELIEVE THEM.

I was naive enough to fall for his lies, and instead of standing up for myself and questioning him, I fell even harder. Then Rhett broke up with me and got right back together with his ex. I was devastated, angry, and I extremely depressed.

I definitely started to nit-pick a lot of things he did, and noticed red flags. I got the courage to stand up for myself more during this time in the midst of depression, until that following February when I fell for him again.

Once again, I got trapped in his spell, but this time it cost me about $10,000. Since I had filed for child support so late, Rhett owed back support. When parents don't pay their checking accounts end are frozen, and that's exactly what happened. He told me about it, so I went to visit him at work, we worked right across the street from each other, and gave him my credit card. I told him that I would figure it out. Rhett told me that he thought he needed to be with me because I took good care of him, and treated him right. I informed him that I wasn't trying to guilt-trip him into being with me, and I was going to do what I did regardless.

The very next morning before work, I went to the child support office and signed away all of the back support debt no questions asked. Rhett asked me if I got it done, I said yes, and sure enough, he told me he loved me and wanted to date again. He invited me over to spend the night at the house he had recently bought. Lily and I went over there, and the next day he broke up with his ex again and we got back together. Once again, I felt like I was on top of the world and that this was going to last.

And once again, God slammed this door right shut, but this time even harder.

Disclaimer: If God shuts a door He wants to stay shut, He will always do that no matter how much pain it causes us. I learned this the hard way, unfortunately.

This second time we dated officially was even shorter than the first time. This time was only a week before something happened.

The weekend after we determined our relationship, you know good ole DTR, we had gone grocery shopping. Prior to this grocery trip, I was feeling funny and I knew something wasn't right. I had never felt this before. So I grabbed some Monistat, thinking I had a yeast infection.

Later that night while we were eating pizza, I got questioned in front of our friends asking why I was feeling so ill. I eventually told

The Greatest Risk of All

him I thought I had a yeast infection. He just sat there and chuckled thankful that I wasn't pregnant again.

This infection lasted longer than I had anticipated, and the medicine wasn't working, so I eventually mustered up the courage to go to the doctor that following Tuesday. He absolutely wanted to know what the outcome was, so I committed to telling him.

The appointment took a turn for the worse. I was told I had herpes. I had blisters everywhere, and I was in so much pain. Since my appointment was on my lunch break, I left there and immediately called Rhett but he wouldn't talk to me about it because he was out to lunch with his co-workers. I was devastated the rest of the afternoon at work, and he ignored me.

Finally at 5 pm, both of us should have been off work at that point, and he still was dodging my phone calls, refusing to talk to me about it. I then did what any self-respecting girl would have done, I called his friend to tell them about it.

Although he was mad, calling his friend worked like a charm. Rhett screamed at me on the other end, saying how dare I say anything to his friends, because that's a pretty slutty thing to do and experience, and it wasn't something I should be proud of. I reminded him of his friends already knowing something was up a few days prior from our conversation in the kitchen, so why did it matter all of a sudden?

Rhett accused me of being the giver, and not the recipient of it, and told me he was breaking up with me because he just needed to be single.

Here I was, crying my eyes out, in pain, telling him how much I loved him and was willing to work through this with him because I wasn't mad at him, and he breaks up with me? I couldn't understand, but as I know now, God will do anything and everything to shut a door that you don't belong in. This way was excruciatingly painful.

After this painful moment, I still let him see Lily once a week, up until that following April. I found out through his friends that he told his girlfriend that if they were to ever have kids, he would look at Lily and consider her a stepchild. This moment was the absolute final straw for me. I told Rhett until further notice he would not see Lily. I blocked his number and moved on with our lives.

This "final straw" only lasted about two months until I saw him driving in his car, looking sad, and I reached out asking him if he would like to see Lily again. I had found out he had been in contact with a lawyer to demand joint custody. I tried to take matters into my own hands by being gracious, and meeting up with him to attempt to come up with our own agreement so we could avoid court costs.

His list of demands seemed simple and something I could deal with so I agreed to everything he requested.

For a couple of years I was okay with everything, up until it was time for Lily to be in school, and that's when it became a living nightmare. We literally fought about everything, it was mostly about money because he was nickle and dime-ing everything and didn't want to pay any more than he already did through child support.

Between health insurance issues, her breaking a couple of bones, and then her being in dance class on his evenings, our fights were endless. I was in a constant state of chaos it seemed. I was always angry with him, and I just questioned what God was doing in my life.

Eventually, he took me to court over her school because we weren't agreeing on the right way to handle it. His motive was money, mine was safety and convenience for her, and it was like pulling teeth to agree.

This court date was extremely depressing for me. He had her old pre-school teacher to testify against me in court, and had pictures of her underwear, accused me of not bathing her, not helping her with her homework, and not feeding her also. My goodness, that was incredibly rough. Plus my lawyer didn't show up either, so I was on my own and I felt attacked.

At this point, I had thoroughly accepted the fact that this was my life, and all I could do was pray for him, and hope that God would change his heart, and even despite all of this, I still wanted to be with him.

I am sure at this point a lot of you are questioning why in the h-e-double hockey sticks I would still pray that God would amend my family and allow me to be with him. But just like God slams doors, I also think God has us stay in a season of despair, mixed with hope, in order to prepare for greater blessings on the other side.

Even after he got engaged, I still prayed that God would bring him and me together, and I still was not losing hope. It took him actually getting married for me to realize that God was permanently shutting that door. You may call me crazy or insane, but I will never give up on hope in what God is trying to accomplish in my life, no matter what the world may show.

{ 10 }

Risk #5: 365 Letters

I'm sure you're thinking who in the heck would write 365 letters?! Trust me, before I did, I thought the same exact thing. How did I get there? Glad you asked!

In October 2015, eight short months after I had my heart broken by my ex and dealt with and std, there was this guy who walked into the bank who was now a partner for our branch. I remember locking eyes with him, thinking he was good-looking, and then glanced down to see a wedding ring. I was pretty disappointed at that moment, but I am sure he was going to be a great addition to our branch.

He was our operations partner, and I had plenty of reasons to talk with him to discuss branch operations. Little did I know the friendship that was going to transpire from our many interactions.

In March 2016, right before my friendship with him really started to flourish, I was at my breaking point with my family. My sister had cussed me out on social media over a hoodie that she saw I was wearing in pictures of mine and Lily's Easter Sunday adventures. Let me preface this by saying my sister tends to be very narcissistic like our mother and is very possessive of all of her items, especially her clothing,

We had had multiple arguments and fallouts over the years over me borrowing her clothing. I never got them dirty, and I really liked what she had. I had told her countless times I would stop, and never really did because I enjoyed wearing some of her stuff. That particular Easter Sunday it was cold, my whole family was in Jamaica, so Lily and I were on our own for typical celebrations. We did an Easter egg hunt outside, and since it was cold, I went to grab a hoodie. I had gone into her room for something, and low and behold there was her old middle school hoodie laying right there in plain sight for me to grab, so I did just that, and then went outside to do the egg hunt then posted about it, without thinking of what ramifications I was about to face.

Shortly after, I was getting very mean and hateful comments on my pictures from my sister about me wearing her hoodie. I was in disbelief, but at this point in my life, I really should have anticipated it.

A few days later, my family arrived home, and my sister was fuming mad at me over this hoodie. She started yelling and screaming at me. I tried to ignore her by staying on my phone and maintaining every single bit of composure I had left. She took my phone right out of my hands which was troubling for Lily to watch. After all, Lily was just one month shy of being four at the time, she had no idea what was going on.

My mom always took my sister's side and excused her poor behavior, but this particular instance took the cake.

The Greatest Risk of All

Since Lily started to freak out about how my sister was treating me, my mom took Lily outside and said "come with me Lily so your aunt can have her way with your mom." I couldn't even believe what I had just heard. I still shudder thinking about this moment. Because after my mom took Lily outside, my sister began to scream at me and got extremely violent. She started to chase me around the house, she shoved me against the wall, and so I slapped her back as hard as I could. She then got angrier and we took our fight outside, it was a huge screaming match, where my mom and my sister called me a slut and a whore.

At that moment, I had had enough and I left the house with Lily and began to look at apartments. I couldn't believe it had to take me to this moment to finally search for an apartment. Especially when the week before that, my mom got in a huge fight with me over a stroller, and I left the house after bursting into a panic attack. Our fight was so bad, I had slammed my door so hard that it broke the doorknob so I was locked in my room. When I left that day to blow off some steam, I was told by my mom "good, don't come back."

I had never had a panic attack before this moment, and I was fully ready to go drive myself into a ditch and kill myself. I had to call everyone I knew to convince myself out of these very destructive thoughts. So after getting into that fight, I was completely done living with my family. So I found an apartment, applied for it, and got approved a day later. And April 1st, 2016 I moved into my very first apartment on my own. It was incredibly scary but I knew I absolutely needed it.

It was also April that my and that guy's, let's call him Brooks, friendship started to flourish, which really made dealing with my family drama that much easier.

We had started to text on and off when his baby was born the month before, but then his wife had a weekend out of town, so that's when he and I really started to talk a lot.

What seemed to be an innocent friendship of us helping each other, quickly became into something on a much more emotional level. We began to confide in each other about our painful pasts. Brooks told me some extremely difficult stories and events that happened in his marriage, and I told him about my family drama, as well as the issues I had with my ex, on top of my desire to be with him, which he couldn't seem to wrap his head around whatsoever.

He had asked me why I would want to be with some guy that had treated me so terribly, and who clearly didn't love me the way that I deserved to be loved. Brooks then told me about all of the wonderful qualities I had in my soul, and how much I meant to him. Which then sent me into grieving over a loss of a dream. He was so upset that he couldn't be there with me the night he sent me into grieving, but I knew it was something I had to do on my own.

Shortly after this, we began to hang out outside of work. Brooks got me flowers which was the start of our love for each other. In two weeks our relationship went from being friends and being there for one another, to telling each other "I love you," and getting tattoos for each other. We couldn't believe how quickly our relationship had grown, and despite how wrong it really was, it seemed so right

The Greatest Risk of All

and so genuine. But like I have said before, God will slam doors in some very painful ways.

That following August, I became really sick. I was struck with a severe UTI and ended up getting my appendix taken out. Brooks came to visit me at the hospital and even took me home when I was finally discharged. Despite the cautious words of others, I was incredibly smitten and was fully convinced that God had made us for each other to save us from very incredibly painful situations.

Since I had two weeks off work, he had taken a vacation day the same week I had my surgery. We went to go hang out by the river and had lunch together at my apartment. It was a very fun-filled afternoon, but it was full of hiding and secrets from his wife. Eventually, the truth was found out that he was not at work like he said he was, and he had to go home to an understandably angry wife. That same weekend, they had gone out of town, and he emailed and called me when he could. At this point, things were on the rocks and he was 75% ready to call it quits with her.

The following Monday when he had gotten back, that's when everything blew up for good.

Usually, Brooks would text me in the morning, drop off his son at daycare, and then he would call me on his hour-long commute to work. This particular morning I knew something was up when I got a text, but never got my usual phone call. I had tried to call and text him multiple times, but no response. My heart began to sink, and I began to panic at what could have possibly been happening. What made it worse was that all of sudden my messages were on "read" status and that had never happened before, plus I got a text from what seemed to be his wife. So I called a mutual friend and coworker of ours. Up until this point, I had not told anyone about what we had.

Our positions in the company could have caused us to be in trouble if work knew about it, so we hid it as much as we could although we weren't as successful as we had thought.

When I called our mutual friend, she told me that he had a doctor's appointment for his son. I told her I knew that wasn't the case, and I needed her to tell me what was actually going on, and not cover it up.

Turns out, his wife had suspicions and looked at his iPad that particular morning which had every single one of our texts on it. I can't imagine how she felt seeing that, but I can only imagine it was extremely painful. He had been deleting our conversations off of his iPhone every day, but his iPad was synced to the cloud and stored all of our messages.

At that moment, I was extremely depressed, uncertain as to why all of this had even happened. I started to question all sorts of things, especially God's plan and reason as to why he and I had met.

What started as grief quickly turned into anger. I became upset at how things were being handled. I got threatening text messages from his wife, and then it went from talking all the time, to only chatting at work, and then to nothing at all. It even got to the point of him only showing up on the days I was off work, or he was leaving about five minutes prior to my start time. Soon enough I was telling people at work about the reality of the situation,

The Greatest Risk of All

and then he was no longer a partner at my branch. This of course caused him to get angry with me.

During my soul searching, I began to pray for answers and reasons. I even started to go back to praying for my ex, hoping that we were still meant to be together and that maybe this other guy was just a distraction from my actual mission all along.

Do I sound crazy yet? If I don't, just wait! Oh, I forgot to tell you, during my summer fling, I also went skydiving for the first time. It was a great experience and a huge risk, but I couldn't commit to writing a whole entire chapter about it. I will say I decided to take the leap of faith because I wanted to let go of all of my pain, and jumping out of a plane seemed like the best way to do it, Turns out, that guy was super concerned for my life and was beside himself when my phone had died and he wasn't hearing from me.

For the next six months, I kept praying that God would guide me and my ex back together, and then June came around when he was getting married. I needed a big distraction, so I played dodgeball with work that same day, and as fate would have it, I broke my wrist. What a wonderful distraction, huh? Sure enough, my ex got married as they had planned, and I was back to square one questioning God and all of the heartbreak He had recently put me through. I was on a roller coaster of emotions, kept trying to put myself out there with men, and got rejected a few times.

Later that year during the fall, I got a random group text from Brooks talking about how he would call the cops. I was shaken with disbelief. Trying to figure out who the third number belonged to in this group chat, I contacted that mutual friend of ours figuring she had the scoop. She said, "oh that's his ex-wife." I was like wait, what?! Ex?! I couldn't believe my ears. At that moment I found out they were getting a divorce. I tried to talk to him about it, and he wanted absolutely nothing to do with me. In the midst of tears, and breaking down mentally and emotionally at work. I cried out to God asking why I found this out, and what He would possibly be asking me to do with this information.

I heard Him tell me to pray for him, and write letters to him. Sure enough, I started that day and began to write letters as long as I had the peace to do so. Which ended up being for a full year! I never thought I would have ended up writing a full year's worth of letters, but sure enough, I did. I would typically write them during my quiet time with God, and tell him how I was praying for him, in addition to telling him about my day. I found it incredibly comforting to pray over him, pray to God about the things going on in my life, and write as well.

When I told people about this, I was told I was absolutely crazy, I had a lot of kickback about it, and ironically enough I found support too. Even though it seemed crazy, I was at peace. I found so much peace during this journey and found out how to be at peace by myself as well. Since I am extremely extroverted, discovering peace being by myself was a huge accomplishment for me.

And I will say, unlike my journey of being a prayer warrior for my ex, when I was on a roller coaster of emotions, I found so much peace while writing to him. I called them "letters to B" because we called each other B.

The Greatest Risk of All

Writing these letters got me through some pretty rough times. That court experience I had mentioned in the previous chapter had occurred right before I started writing these letters, but then when I had issues afterward with my ex or even with family, I found peace in writing and praying. Sleepless and depressing nights turned into peaceful evenings of writing these letters, praying, and soaking up all of my time alone.

I even had an idea of publishing the letters as my very first book, but I am very thankful that God guided me to write and publish this story as my first one instead.

{ 11 }

Risk #6: Kidney Donation

To say that God works in mysterious ways would be the understatement of life. I have often said that I wish God would smack me in the face with some signs, and for this particular risk, He had done just that.

Like all the other risks I have talked about, this also had somewhat of a backstory.

A few years before I had seen this sign, I remember hearing a church service from a lady at our previous church, and she talked about how God told her to give a kidney to a lady she was in a small group with. For some reason, I have never forgotten about this message, but I never really did anything about it because for one, I didn't know if God was really speaking to me to do it, and two, no one came knocking on my door in need of a kidney.

Also prior to this, I had already had knee surgery in 2015, got rid of my appendix in 2016, and then said "see-ya" to my non-working gallbladder in 2017 after being sick for six months, So after all what was one more organ to get rid of, and what was one more surgery? It was actually a running joke at my work about what or-

The Greatest Risk of All

gan I was going to get rid of next, and sure enough, my kidney was next in line to go.

So here I was, roughly about six months into writing the letters. I was healthy, after being sick for the majority of the previous year, owned my own condo for a year at this point, and then low and behold on my normal drive to work, I see a sign on the side of the road. The sign said "Greg needs a kidney," and underneath there was a phone number to call.

I can't even explain the way I was feeling besides my heart was pounding out of my chest, my hands were sweaty, and then I tried to work but I just couldn't shake this feeling of what this sign had said.

I began to question God, and ask Him "are you REALLY trying to tell me to get rid of my kidney?" This just can't be. But I absolutely could not work and I couldn't focus straight whatsoever. So I began to text pretty much every friend of mine on my phone that would pray for me while I sorted these emotions and thoughts out. I was asking God if I could just work and think about this later, but I wasn't able to.

My job at the time had this program where we had to go get a fitness test with a nurse, bike on a like machine, and talk about our health. This was for our health insurance so we could get so much money back each paycheck, and ironically enough my appointment to do this was this same exact day. Which meant I had to leave my office to go to this appointment, which then meant on my way back I drove past this sign, once again.

This time was different, I decided to use the good ole call a friend method, talk things out, and then when I was driving past the sign, I stopped and got the number. Then I pulled back into the parking lot, hung up the phone, walked inside, and asked God politely if He would let me work and I promised Him I would call that number as soon as I was leaving work.

Let me just tell you, if you make promises to God, He will not, and I repeat, He will NOT let you forget it.

Sure enough, I got to work like normal, and I almost forgot to call, but I remember walking out those doors and feeling a heavy brick just hit me reminding me to call that phone number I took down. So I called it and it connected me straight to a lady at Christ Hospital named Tricia Monson who happened to be the kidney donor coordinator. I was relieved I wasn't calling some stranger, but I was still nervous as could be.

She only worked during the day until about 3 pm, so working at a bank and leaving around 5 pm each day, I had to leave a voicemail. I was actively holding back tears, and basically told her I felt like I was supposed to donate a kidney, and would like more information on how to get started.

The very next day, she called me back. I answered with hesitation and tears, but I knew I was doing what I needed to do.

She started the conversation by asking me how I was feeling, what led me to this, and then began to talk to me about the process and how it would go. The very first thing I had to do was to submit paperwork. I was able to put Greg on my paperwork, but she said that he was actually in the process of receiving a transplant. Unfortunately, transplants aren't always successful though, because the donor can back out, or the transplant could be rejected as well. She

The Greatest Risk of All

continued to tell me that if the transplant is successful, I could become an altruistic donor (a donor with no specific recipient, one is anonymous, and starts a chain of surgeries), or if the transplant is not successful, we could start setting me up to be the donor for Greg.

Without hesitation to all of this, I simply told her I was in, and fully ready to get started.

The next steps were receiving the paperwork to fill out to become a donor, and she said I was going to have them in my mail in a couple of days.

Meanwhile, I was still writing those letters and felt completely called to get the guy I was writing to, a Father's Day gift since it was quickly approaching. After all, I knew he was going through a lot, and I wanted to let him know I was thinking about him.

It worked out to where I submitted the paperwork for being a donor and mailed off his gift the same exact day, and man did I feel good! I felt I was on top of the world.

But like I have talked about, every risk we take can have different outcomes.

Apparently, my gift to that guy, made him angry, and he apparently threw it away. I found this out because my manager decided to talk to me about what was going on with him, and I told her I wasn't giving up, but I was fine with him throwing my gift away and acting crazy. It just made me want to write more, pray more, and fight harder.

I also felt incredibly crazy about donating a kidney, until my manager talked to her mom about her dad being in need of a kidney, then I felt I could confide in her and talk with her about it.

Months passed by, and I finally received a phone call about what my next steps were about becoming a kidney donor. I was told that Greg received his transplant successfully, and I was going to start the process of being an altruistic donor. I couldn't have been more nervous, yet more excited at the same time.

During the beginning of this process, it was pretty difficult to find my support system. I got a decent amount of backlash from girls in my small group, and I wasn't ready to talk to my family yet about it, and I am honestly glad I waited. Yet God still found ways to provide me with the support I needed.

I had recently picked up another part-time job to earn some extra cash, so I was too busy to be overwhelmed with feelings anyway. Then a friend of mine from church told me about this guy who just had donated his kidney in February of that year. He also worked at a bank, and ironically enough the week before we met in person, he had just moved into the condos that were two buildings up from mine. Seriously! God is amazing and works in miraculous ways.

I couldn't even believe what I had found out, but I was glad to have him as a support system and friend because I very much needed all the advice and information I could get.

The Greatest Risk of All

Another thing I found out was that Tricia was actually a cousin-in-law of a really good friend of mine, whose dad also dealt with kidney failure and had eventually received a transplant as well. So many pieces were stitching together to show me God absolutely had His hand in this, It was undeniable.

I had my beginning appointment date to start the very lengthy testing to prove to the donor team that I was fit in all ways to donate. It was set to happen in mid-September, and for 24 hours prior to this appointment, I had to pee in a jug so they could run tests on it.

A few days before this appointment, I had gone to see Lauren Daigle in concert with a friend of mine. I was experiencing a ton of tooth pain, and then what also happened that same night was something unthinkable.

In my senior year of high school, I shadowed the gym teacher and we became very close friends. We ended up working together at the Red's stadium, and we connected on some very deep levels. Well, it turns out that that same day, she ended up having a stillborn and was in critical condition. Her kidneys started to fail, and she had to have a lot of life-saving surgeries. I couldn't believe what I was witnessing., so I reached out to her sister and told her that if for some reason her sister ended up needing a kidney, I am about to start the process to become a donor, and I would have been happy to hold out and save my kidney for her.

At this moment, I received yet another confirmation from God that I was exactly where I needed to be, and was doing exactly what He had called me to do.

The following Monday it was time for my first round of testing. A lot went into this. I had to get an EKG, had to get blood work, basically be drained right under the legal limit, do other basic testings, and then also meet with a social worker.

The meeting with the social worker lasted an hour. I had to talk about everything, and I mean everything. During that conversation, I could once again tell that I was where I was supposed to be because I felt nothing but crazy spiritual attacks from the enemy, Satan. I explained the rape, the issues with my mom, the painful experience with my daughter's bio dad, and so much more. Amazingly enough, I was able to have a full-blown conversation about every bit of this without shedding one single tear.

I got asked if I had ever had sexual experiences with another woman, multiple people, etc. I am not sure how this was relevant, but I felt a little violated.

During this encounter, the worker tried to tell me that I was not in the right position to donate a kidney because I had so much going on. I told him I understood, but I was so ready to do this. I knew God would be with me, protect me, and God calls the people who seem to be the "least qualified," and equips them to do what He has asked them to do. I knew that God was going to prevail and give me everything I needed to complete the task even though the worker didn't seem to be so certain.

He continued to ask me more details about the court date I had had with Lily's bio dad back in 2016, and I told him that I was told to take parenting and co-parenting classes but I hadn't done them

The Greatest Risk of All

yet. He also asked me that if I was so certain God would be there for me during this surgery, then where was He when I got raped and experienced all that other turmoil in my past? I simply replied that God was always there, and helped me get through my pain.

The conversation ended, and I walked out to the parking garage, got in my car, and began to bawl my eyes out. It had been quite a while since I had encountered a spiritual attack like that, and it made me want to fight even harder to make this happen. I was not about to give up. After all, I had already been told I was crazy, that God shouldn't ask me to do this, questioned if I was even hearing God correctly, etc. I was at the point that the thought of not doing it made me physically ill.

Every Thursday, the people who were on my donation team would meet. Tricia was my main helper, and she met with everyone who tested me to determine if I was qualified to go to the next step, including that social worker. I will never forget the pit in my stomach when I got a call later in the week about how the social worker deemed me unfit to continue the process since my life was crazy, and it didn't seem to him an appropriate time to do such an extreme surgery. I replied I was ready, and knew I had to do it. After going back and forth, he basically told me to work on getting the parenting and co-parenting classes done, and then he would re-evaluate.

I received some help from my co-worker at the time trying to find these classes. I made several phone calls and so many of the classes were in person on evenings I was supposed to have Lily, and it was supposed to go on for about 8 weeks or so, and they weren't even starting for another few months. I began to research other options because I knew in my heart I couldn't wait that long.

After a lot of research, I finally found an online class that was $25 and it satisfied both classes I had to do! It was 4 hours long, so I went home that night, registered for it, took the online course in about 30 minutes, and let it time out the rest of the 3.5 hours while I sat there on my bed and watched Netflix. This was one of the best decisions I felt I had ever made. Once it was done, I printed out the certificate, emailed it off, and told him I was done with what he had asked.

The following week they met again, I received yet another phone call from him trying to convince me to wait 6 months or so. I politely told him that my life was not going to be any different in 6 months than it is now. I am working 2 jobs, doing the very best that I can, and I wanted to get this done. I also told him I had satisfied those classes he requested, and I would like to continue. He then gave me his approval and told me they would meet again and talk about it.

They met and called me again after, and this time I got the final approval!! I was so relieved. I was now in the position of waiting to get scheduled for surgery, and I had nothing left to do until about a week or so before my surgery.

During this time they also had to get approval from the urologist because I did get a bladder scope in 2017 to make sure nothing was wrong because I felt like I was peeing a heck of a lot, and I wanted to see what was up. By God's grace, that was completely cleared, nothing wrong, and I was in the clear to donate my kidney.

The Greatest Risk of All

Weeks turned into months of waiting. I was filled with anticipation just wanting to donate a kidney already. I have never once been so excited to go through surgery, but here I was just talking to everyone I knew except my family about how I was so determined to get this done.

I finally received a phone call in mid-January letting me know they were going to have my surgery scheduled for February 5th. At that moment, I knew it was time to break the news to my family. I sent a group text to everyone, and then all hell broke loose.

My parents weren't exactly thrilled with me, and neither were my siblings. Except for my older brother. He was one that had my back and let everyone know it was truly my decision.

The week prior to my surgery, I had to go back to the hospital to get a round of final testing, and my parents wanted to come with me. It was a very full day, with lots of tears, and emotions. I was hoping that after this day of testing, and having conversations with the surgeon, my parents would be more on board, however, I was very wrong.

I almost feel that it made everything worse. Neither of them was thrilled about it, and no amount of information could calm them down either. At that point, I knew I just had to pray.

When I left the hospital that afternoon, I went to work, and that evening I had a date. It gave me something to look forward to!

I am not one that has had success with online dating, but this guy I actually added on Facebook because I saw we went to the same church. I thought he was attractive, we talked a lot, and then we had a coffee date set for that evening.

While we were out, I told him about donating a kidney, and I told him about the 365 letters I had written and BURNED the night before. I wanted to be fully prepared for this date, and having 365 letters sitting at my house while I was trying to give a guy a chance, didn't seem right to me. I told him about all of that, and I told him I felt that our outing was a divine appointment from God. We talked until the place closed, and he wanted to pray over me and my upcoming surgery. I was so excited for my chance to see him again, and I continued to talk to him sparingly after the fact, but then later found out while in the hospital that he began dating another girl.

It was the weekend right before my surgery, and I was working. I had received countless text messages and phone calls during this weekend all from family begging and urging me not to donate a kidney. Asking me to go to counseling, asking me to update my will, asking me to reconsider until I was married, or even asking me to wait 6 months while they came to terms with it. I was not having it.

One conversation, in particular, was with my sister, and she was asking me to admit the fact that I could die, leave Lily stranded with an abusive dad, and leave my family behind. I am a big believer when it comes to speaking things into existence and allowing my mind to stay positive (especially right before surgery) because I feel our mind is our greatest asset and if we allow fear or thoughts of death to creep in while we are under, we have a greater chance of not making it out. So I told her I was not going to say I had a

The Greatest Risk of All

chance of dying, and I would definitely make it out on the other side.

I received so many horrible text messages from family that weekend at work that I burst into a panic attack. I was being told so many hateful things, and I couldn't take it anymore. I hit my breaking point, called my parents to yell at them and tell them how heartbroken I was. I began to ask the community around me to take care of Lily while I was under and recovering as well since I was told I could no longer receive their help with her. I was so distraught, I sat on the floor in the corner and just shook and wept. I was at a loss and didn't know what to do anymore.

I am so grateful I was at work during this time, surrounded by people, otherwise, I don't know what I would have done.

The rest of the weekend I took the space I needed to heal, decompress and remove stress from my life. The following Monday I spent the day working, then went home, took care of Lily, and then eventually took her to my parent's house. I ended up staying there way longer than anticipated because I had a long heart to heart conversation with my dad, and afterward, he gave me a letter and told me he apologized if there was anything in there that I was mad about, to not hate him because he rewrote it about 20 times trying to perfect it. But after our conversation, he felt much better about my decision.

The next morning it was time for my surgery, so my friend and neighbor picked me up. I told my roommate at the time I was leaving and she yelled at me and told me she didn't care and didn't want to know when I was out of surgery either. Up until the Sunday right before this, she and I had been getting along just fine. She was one of my Airbnb guests that had been there since November. Something changed out of nowhere but I knew I didn't have time to deal with it either, so I went on my merry way to the hospital.

I stayed there a total of 2 days and had several visitors. One of them was my best friend at the time, and she had met one of my guy friends that night too. He was of course infatuated with her, but she was dating someone else. She was also the one who took me home from the hospital and visited me frequently while I recovered. I was and still am very thankful for her, even though we had a falling out not too long after this.

The following weekend after my surgery, was one of the toughest parts of my recovery. The roommate I liked was gone out of town for work, I was stuck with the one who yelled at me, and she had me sign a contract for her to stay there while I was on high-end medication. She had asked to stay there for a full year, and I don't even remember what it said, or what date I had put on it. All I knew was she wasn't going to pay me money until I signed it, and I was desperate. So I went with it.

This same weekend my mom had taken Lily to a dance competition out of town that I so badly wanted to go to, but I was in no position to handle a car ride let alone a weekend away from home. Thank goodness I didn't go because I ended up puking all over my bathroom floor from lack of food and just the right amount of medication, and I have never experienced so much pain before. Even recovering from a C-section along with laughing/sneezing did not compare to gut-wrenching vomiting. I felt like my insides were on fire.

The Greatest Risk of All

After a few weeks, I started to move around more and had to get a check-up at the doctor, and during this time I started to have issues with my mean roommate. It started to become awkward to go home because she was being mean, and somewhat abusive over text, and she would flat out ignore me and give my daughter mean stares, etc. I did not feel safe whatsoever. So I did whatever I could to get out of my house. I ended up breaking down and consulting a lawyer about her too, because she told me she was not going to move out because she had a contract with me that allowed her to stay there until February 2020. Once again, I was at a loss on what to do.

The lawyer route was going to be so expensive, so I ended up going the route of getting a letter typed up from my work and posting on the door that gave her a 30-day notice to get out of my house. She left the notice up, and from that day forward I prayed that she would be out by my birthday, which she was!

St. Patty's day rolled around and I had gone out with the girl and guy that both visited me at the hospital. I have this poor habit of giving in to whatever my friends want, allowing them to be happy even if it meant I was taking a risk of being shoved to the curb. Which had happened before in college, and started to happen during this time as well.

It started with the three of us hanging out, and then they started to hang out together behind my back while I was still on sick leave, and then when I got back to work it got way worse. Not too long after, he had a surgery he didn't tell us about, and she started to think something was up with him, and then we had both agreed not to talk to him especially after he had asked me for my prescription meds. She of course didn't go along with that, and she continued to see him despite my request. I told her, I didn't care to be friends with him anymore since he wasn't making amends, and I honestly didn't want to hear about him either, so I told her she had to choose between us. Some may call it petty, I call it a boundary for me.

After I was pretty broken by this experience, I met up with one of my friends and told her about this, and at that moment she had told me I had abandonment issues. Not physical abandonment, but emotional abandonment. I was blown away, and I knew God was talking through her to me.

The very next week I got "I am worthy" tattooed on my arm, and I even started to take a leap with online dating again, met some guys, got my heart broken once again. Thankfully during this time my Brazilian sister had come to visit and helped me deal with being rejected yet again, and my cool roommate was with me a few more weeks while I was going through this, and she helped me too. Both of them were very beneficial to me and still are to this day.

It was the last weekend of May, and it was time for a mutual friend's wedding. Both that girl and I went to it. I had a date lined up, but I got rejected by him, so I decided to take another girl with me and make it a girl's night. The girl who was seeing my best guy friend ended up taking one of her best guy friends. Prior to this night, I had asked her if she could set us up, and she blatantly refused and was mad at me up until the evening we were at the wedding. She gave me the cold shoulder, but I still introduced myself to him. I figured if she wasn't going to help, I would do it myself. I was

The Greatest Risk of All

confident, I thought he was attractive, and I put myself out there, so much so that I later added him on Facebook, but sadly he never accepted it.

A couple of days after this wedding I got my little ginger back but this time with a cast all the way up her leg. She had broken her tibia the Wednesday before this weekend, and I was heartbroken. I had felt I had a series of bad events, but then on the very last day of May, something happened that changed the rest of my life forever.

{ 12 }

Risk #7: Finding Love

On May 31st, 2019, work started out as it had always had. I had just got up to use the bathroom, and when I walked out I saw this handsome man in need of opening a new bank account. I had just seen him not too long ago, and I remember seeing that he had an account already with us and it was joint with another woman. Which was highly disappointing because I always found him very attractive, but I was respectful.

Sure enough this day, the day after his birthday, Patrick Sean Nash, was in to open a new bank account. I could barely tell you what all we were talking about because I was definitely excited. I just know he told me why they were now separated and in the process of getting a divorce. He also talked about his kids a lot, and Lily had just broken her tibia, so of course, I was a hot mess discussing my crazy situation with my ex and turns out the whole time he was talking about his dogs.

"Ah come on you idiot," I said to myself. I could not even believe I thought he was talking about two one-year-old sons, instead of dogs, but I sure did! I am very prone to being blonde, so this shouldn't surprise many.

The Greatest Risk of All

The absolute crazy thing was, that a month or so before this, I had applied and interviewed for another chance at a promotion that I really wanted and was in desperate need of or so I thought. Fortunately for me, that door was slammed shut in my face. I didn't realize it at the time, but this turned out to be a huge blessing from God. I had also just transferred to the branch I was at a year before too. So had I received any promotion I applied for or worked at my other branch that day, or even permanent, I would have never met this guy that God happily walked through the door of my work.

I was also at the point in my banking career where I was extremely tired of doing the same thing over and over again, especially opening new accounts. I was informed a year or so prior to not discuss my personal life with anyone anymore because apparently, it led to negativity or customers didn't appreciate it. I am glad I took the words of "wisdom" with a grain of salt and continued to be myself despite what I was advised and threatened with. I very much find so much use in being vulnerable and transparent with people you come in contact with. You never know when you could be meeting your forever best friend, husband, or someone you could influence greatly with your story.

At the time when I met this handsome man, I was in a position where I thought I needed to stop dating. In the months leading up to this moment, I had put myself back on a dating website, and met some men who treated me horrible. I was tired of the emotional roller coaster I was continually experiencing, and I was just about done.

I am also certain that this was one of the longest account opening encounters I had had in a while. The whole conversation seemed so fluent, and he swears that God did the talking for him because he's not one to flirt like that.

After our conversation came to a close, he told me to take note of his phone number. I ended up texting him later, which he was thrilled about and didn't anticipate. He asked me to go on a date with him as well and asked when the earliest I could meet up was.

During this time in my life, I was working my full-time bank job and part-time serving and bartending at our local movie theatre. I also had joint custody with my ex so I had Lily every other weekend, and Mondays and Tuesdays, so all the days I didn't have her, I was working. Needless to say, the thought of adding dating to the mix stressed me out, but I made it possible because I was willing to take this chance.

I finally agreed to have a lunch date on my lunch break in the middle of the week at a local restaurant. He showed up with roses, and he was very nervous, as was I, however, it was still very enjoyable. Then the following weekend, I didn't have Lily so we went to Main Event to play video games and go bowling together after I finished working at the movie theatre that night. We had a blast!

A week or so later, we finally declared it official. I had gone to my girlfriend's house for wine and had a nice girl's weekend. And I ended up confessing my love for him via text that evening, and we defined our relationship as officially dating.

When I had talked about everything with Story, I was pacing around in her kitchen telling her I was unsure and didn't know

The Greatest Risk of All

what to do. Because of her, I took the plunge to tell him I loved him and wanted to be with him. We are forever grateful for her!

The beginning of July was full of adventures. We went kayaking on the 4th, then to Cedar Point the weekend after, which is hands down one of our favorite adventures. Later on that month we went on our first vacation together with Lily to his favorite spot in Florida. It was much needed and so wonderful! It was very enjoyable even though I didn't handle things very well. I didn't know how to receive love and because of that we almost broke. up because of that. The trip brought up some painful memories and conversations.

Thankfully, God is sovereign and helped me heal, in addition to allowing us to move forward. We started to talk about the future! By the end of July I was picking out a ring I wanted, and he bought it not too long after.

The rest of our summer was filled with more adventures, countless date nights, and planning for our future. In addition to continual conversations about whether or not I was truly ready to settle down and get married. I felt in my heart I was, but I also kept making excuses to him thinking I had to pay off all of my debt I incurred without dragging him into the mess I felt I created. He kept assuring me otherwise that I didn't have to have it all together, even if I felt like I did. He told me he would take on every single thing I had, and be willing to work with me through it as a team.

September 20th-21st, we went camping at Red River Gorge. The following day after we got back, we went to church like normal. That afternoon he put me on a scavenger hunt of all the places that were important to us, and left notes along with Bible verses about marriage, to end me up at the meeting point of Alt Park in Cincinnati where he finally popped the question. I was so excited to be engaged to the man of my dreams!! Ironically enough, we had already decided what date we wanted to get married, and we had an appointment with a wedding planner at a hotel to view the place we wanted to have our wedding reception.

The rest of 2019 was filled with holidays together, planning for our future, and for our wedding. We announced to all of our friends and family and started asking people to be in our wedding. Both of us were super excited to start this new adventure together!

Then 2020 happened and everything that year decided to bring.

January 2020, he had just got a job offer from his current job to become the in-plant manager at the new plant in Las Vegas, Nevada. Other offers had come and gone prior to this, but Vegas was the one that just wouldn't go away no matter how many times he had denied it. When he approached me with the idea, I was completely down and told him I was all for it! But I was also very hesitant.

He absolutely loves to hunt, so a week later, he decided to go hunting, and that was his time to communicate with God and determine if this was the path we were supposed to go down. After he felt peace about it, he called his manager and asked what he would get for going out there. They went through everything, and he was on his way to accepting this new job.

The Greatest Risk of All

As part of the acceptance process, his company had to fly us out to find a new place to live, check out the plant, the area, etc. So we went to Vegas Super Bowl weekend, found an apartment, visited the plant, and then decided to elope while we were there.

You see, in order to move to Vegas, we had to change the custody agreement I had with Rhett for my daughter because I was only allowed to live so far from him with the arrangement we had. And like you have read prior, I am sure you can imagine I was pretty well spent on dealing with him anyway. We were hoping for Patrick to adopt her once we were married. Our original plan was to start the process in June, the same month we were getting married, but since we eloped on February 1st, 2020, we were able to get the ball rolling on the adoption the same month. Although I have to admit, eloping before our wedding wasn't exactly the plan I had in mind, it definitely helped move things forward in an amazing way.

After we got back from Vegas, we didn't really tell a whole lot of people we eloped since we were trying to keep things special for the wedding we were already planning. We jumped right into meeting with an attorney to start the adoption process, and we ended the month with going to Disney World as a family, while I ran the half marathon and 10k, which had been on my bucket list for quite some time.

All of these events brought so much excitement, followed by an exceptional amount of tears. As soon as we got back from Disney, he had to turn around pack, and prepare to drive out to Vegas. He had to be out there starting March 1st, so that meant months of distance and dealing with everything else 2020 decided to bring.

REBEKAH R. NASH

Prior to him moving, I was experiencing a variety of emotions. I was nervous, anxious, depressed, and that only increased after he moved away.

Suddenly my grandmother passed away, the world shut down, and then my cousin passed away after that. This all happened within a month of him leaving. I was mad and angry that I had to deal with so much after my husband just moved 2000 miles away from us. I was also stressed about the wedding, and the adoption process too. I just wanted one thing that I felt had been resolved, or that I had control over, but I had no choice but to give it all and surrender every bit of it to God.

The beginning of April brought yet another new set of challenges. I was unable to attend my cousin's funeral. Lily and I were about ready to go visit Patrick in Vegas. I told my work about it, not thinking anything of it, but then the travel restriction came about, and I went anyway. I politely told them I didn't have to say what I did on my vacation, but because I even told them my original plans, I had to prove I "didn't go" in order to come back to work. This brought on weeks of anxiety, frustration, and anger. I battled with the company and I was in complete disbelief that they didn't see visiting my husband as essential. But I wasn't about to put work in front of my family. I needed time with my husband, as it was short anyway. We only got to see each other every two weeks.

After my two weeks of quarantine, it was my birthday, which meant he came back again to see us and celebrate our birthdays. Then someone called HR on me, and I got in trouble, yet again. I had to take two more weeks off work.

The Greatest Risk of All

I knew already I would be quitting this job because I knew we were going to be moving in the summer. Prior to all of this, I had already experienced so many problems with the people I was working with. They did not like my character or the emotions I was dealing with, so I knew it was time to leave sooner than later. So after the second quarantine, I put in my resignation and said goodbye. What really blew my mind, was that the manager I worked with for 8 years, didn't even acknowledge me leaving. Didn't give me a hug, or even a wave goodbye, not even a last word. It was insane, and I still to this day have nightmares about it occasionally. I guess this is something I need to really focus on healing from since I was let down in ways beyond what I ever imagined.

Hello, May! Yet another month full of challenges. We had season passes to amusement parks we loved, and neither of them was opened. Which was a total letdown since we were very much looking forward to a summer with adventure, and that went out the window.

At the beginning of May, I continued to feel anxious about our wedding approaching the next month, because things were not getting better, only worse. However, he was able to come home in the middle of May for us to go on a little weekend getaway to Cumberland falls to celebrate Mother's Day. This time he was actually able to stay for a full week! We were excited and it was so needed after not seeing each other much.

After our week together, it was exactly a month prior to our wedding, and I was really freaking out. I started to call several venues in Ohio since the restrictions were better over there than in Kentucky. We found the perfect venue that fit our budget. Then brought the entire change of our menu, new table covers, new napkins, new setting, new seating chart, new everything.

Because of the change, I sent out mass texts, and Facebook notifications to people coming since I wasn't about to send out new wedding invitations, and everything was rocking and rolling again, yet stressful once again.

Later that month we celebrated Patrick's birthday when he was in town again, and then I didn't get to see him until our wedding weekend.

Wedding month, finally! Even though I wasn't able to see him for 3 weeks, I had a lot to do to keep me occupied. Dress fitting, finalizing wedding details, and then my bachelorette party the weekend before our wedding. It was a lot to do in so little time, but I got it all done, and our wedding actually turned out way better than we originally planned. Very exciting to say the least!

The week of our wedding, the tux place was still not open, so we had no idea what that was going to look like. Turns out the place was going out of business, but still sent us all the suits and shoes that were ordered for the wedding, and everyone got to keep them. We had them delivered in a huge box the Wednesday before our wedding, and everything was working out at the very last second. We even got to squeeze in a last-minute dance rehearsal the day before our wedding, which was great.

Our wedding on June 20, 2020, was absolutely perfect. It was when we announced the adoption of Lily. The venue we landed was

The Greatest Risk of All

even more perfect and more beautiful than everything else we could have planned for or imagined. It is truly a day and a time we will never forget, and we received TONS of compliments. It was amazing and perfect in every single way.

The following month was nothing short of crazy. Patrick had to leave to go back to Vegas the Monday after our wedding. I wasn't going to see him for yet another two weeks for our honeymoon.

Just like our wedding, we had all these plans for our honeymoon, that completely got obliterated. We were originally supposed to go to Punta Cana, but our passports were still not in yet. So a week before, I contacted the resort, and sure enough, they were going to be closed until October. I canceled those reservations then booked a resort in Clear Water, Florida for our honeymoon. It was cheaper and turned out wonderful. We had the very best time, and I wouldn't have had it any other way!

Once we got back, we finished packing everything in the condo, About a week later we packed up the truck and U-Haul and made our journey out to Vegas where we are living together as a family now.

Since we have been here, Lily's adoption was finalized in September, we celebrated the holidays together as our small family, and decided to end 2020 with a bang by finding out we were pregnant! Our little baby was due in July 2021, and we couldn't wait!

2020 has definitely given us many challenges along the way. We have experienced every single life change possible this year, and we are extremely blessed!

… { 13 }

Surrender: The Greatest Risk of All

Well, friends, we have reached the end of the story. I am sure you are all wondering that out of all the risks I talked about, which one is the greatest? My answer is simply, surrender. I am not referring to surrendering to an enemy, waving the white flag. I am referring to laying down all that I have and hold dear in this life, at the feet of Christ. I am talking about absolutely surrendering my entire life to Him.

Everything I have explained and discussed in the previous chapters would have never been possible without God. Because of Him, I have learned what it means to be content, how to have peace, and I found the love He chose to put in my path. He has graciously blessed me above what I possibly deserve, and I am so incredibly thankful and humbled.

I originally accepted Christ when I was 5 years old, with the help of my neighbor. Then 20 years later I got baptized for the second time, and it actually meant something to me. At that moment I truly understood the washing away of my past and being able to see the wonderful future He had for me, even though I didn't have all the pieces together.

The Greatest Risk of All

The November after Patrick and I got engaged, we ran a full marathon together with strength truly coming from God, and then the same weekend I had the honor of baptizing him as well. None of this would have been possible without serving God, and fully committing my life to follow Him.

You may ask, how is this risky? Well, because when you say yes to God, you say no to pride, to fear, to worry, to cautiousness. You say no to your body because it is His. I said yes to God, and promised Him I would do anything, and He certainly has not let me forget it. But the best thing of it all is that He blesses His followers tenfold. You could not possibly receive all that this life has to give if you don't surrender to Christ fully. It is well worth it, friend. I promise!

If my story isn't enough of a testament about God rescuing and forming beauty from total destruction of ashes, then I encourage you to find other people who have walked the path of destruction and have found light.

My husband once suffered an addiction, and because of God, he is almost 9 years sober. Our elopement anniversary is actually the anniversary of his sobriety. Which I think is a total miracle, and so amazing. His story is a hard and rough one, but He is alive and well because of God. My hope and prayer are that he, along with all of you, would be passionate and confident enough about the story God has given you. No matter the pain, no matter the skeletons, no matter how dark your journey is or was. Because someone can always learn from what you have been through, and the very best testimonies come from speaking about your failures and that dark path you once were on and how you've overcome.

Father God,

I lift all of my readers up to you right now and ask that you would give them the courage to completely surrender and fully say yes to You in everything You ask of them. I ask that you give them the confidence in You to share their story, and seek You and Your mission above all else. I pray that You put the right and best people in their life to help them continue on their journey, and move forward in every way possible, even when they feel there is no more hope. I pray that You continue to help me be an influence to others, and use this book, and my story, Your story, for Your glory alone. I love you.

Amen.

Remember: No matter where you are in this life, your story is not over yet, and the adventure has just begun!

To my loving Heavenly Father:

Thank you for giving me this amazing journey to write about. Even though I couldn't see it at the time, you have absolutely used every bit of heartache, trial, difficulty, and blessing you have sent my way, ultimately leading to a great story to use to inspire others.

I am so thankful for all of the beautiful ways you have blessed me, and I absolutely would be nothing in this life without you rescuing me and loving me endlessly. I love you!

To my wonderful husband:

Patrick, wow, I am in awe that this dream is coming to life. Ever since I knew you, I have talked about this, and because of you, I have had the freedom to make this happen. I am so grateful God brought you to me in perfect time, and I am so thankful you are a part of this beautiful story! Thank you for loving me the way God loves me, and thank you for all of the ways you have pursued me. I love you today, yesterday, and for all of the years, we have together on this earth. You are my forever love and best friend!

To my amazing editor/publisher:

I am so thankful I met you, and without you, this dream wouldn't have happened! Thank you for all of your hard work, and your beautiful friendship! Much love to you and our mutual friend, Amy, for helping this friendship flourish! You have such an amazing talent. I absolutely look forward to how God uses our talents together to impact more people in this lifetime!

Simply Lynne Photography

Rebekah Nash, formerly known as Rebekah Hill, was born and raised in Northern Kentucky. She attended Calvary Christian School from Kindergarten through Senior year. Then continued her education at Northern Kentucky University. Rebekah graduated from NKU with a bachelor's in Communication Studies and a minor in Organizational Leadership in May 2013.

What she values most in this life is her relationship with God, her husband, two daughters, her family, and friends. She currently lives in Vegas with her family and is fulfilling her dream of being an author, stay-at-home mom, homeschooling their eldest daughter, and working remotely as a customer service representative for a furniture company.

Prior to living in Vegas, she worked in Kentucky as a banker for a total of 8 years. In 2016, she won the top banker award in her region. Although banking wasn't for her long term, what she enjoyed most in that career was helping others feel financially free and accomplishing their dreams. She has further used this experience to help her family and friends accomplish similar goals.

Her favorite things to do are writing, traveling, staying active, and enjoying relaxing evenings watching movies with her husband.

Email: rebekahrnash@gmail.com
Instagram: @rebekahrnash
Facebook: Rebekah R Nash

www.ingramcontent.com/pod-product-compliance
Lightning Source LLC
Chambersburg PA
CBHW050254301025
34736CB00044B/2768